Introduction to Webometrics: Quantitative Web Research for the Social Sciences

Synthesis Lectures on Information Concepts, Retrieval, and Services

Editor
Gary Marchionini, *University of North Carolina, Chapel Hill*

Introduction to Webometrics: Quantitative Web Research for the Social Sciences
Michael Thelwall
2009

Automated Metadata in Multimedia Information Systems: Creation, Refinement, Use in Surrogates, and Evaluation
Michael G. Christel
2009

Exploratory Search: Towards New Search Horizons
Ryen W. White and Resa A. Roth
2009

Reference in a Digital Age
R. David Lankes
2009

Introduction to Webometrics: Quantitative Web Research for the Social Sciences
Michael Thelwall

ISBN: 978-3-031-01133-7   paperback

ISBN: 978-3-031-02261-6   ebook

DOI: 10.1007/978-3-031-02261-6

A Publication in the Springer series

SYNTHESIS LECTURES ON INFORMATION CONCEPTS, RETRIEVAL, AND SERVICES #4

Lecture #4

Series Editor: Gary Marchionini, University of North Carolina, Chapel Hill

Series ISSN Pending

Introduction to Webometrics: Quantitative Web Research for the Social Sciences

Michael Thelwall
University of Wolverhampton

SYNTHESIS LECTURES ON INFORMATION CONCEPTS, RETRIEVAL, AND SERVICES #4

ABSTRACT

Webometrics is concerned with measuring aspects of the web: web sites, web pages, parts of web pages, words in web pages, hyperlinks, web search engine results. The importance of the web itself as a communication medium and for hosting an increasingly wide array of documents, from journal articles to holiday brochures, needs no introduction. Given this huge and easily accessible source of information, there are limitless possibilities for measuring or counting on a huge scale (e.g., the number of web sites, the number of web pages, the number of blogs) or on a smaller scale (e.g., the number of web sites in Ireland, the number of web pages in the CNN web site, the number of blogs mentioning Barack Obama before the 2008 presidential campaign). This book argues that it can be useful for social scientists to measure aspects of the web and explains how this can be achieved on both a small and large scale. The book is intended for social scientists with research topics that are wholly or partly online (e.g., social networks, news, political communication) and social scientists with offline research topics with an online reflection, even if this is not a core component (e.g., diaspora communities, consumer culture, linguistic change). The book is also intended for library and information science students in the belief that the knowledge and techniques described will be useful for them to guide and aid other social scientists in their research. In addition, the techniques and issues are all directly relevant to library and information science research problems.

KEYWORDS

webometrics, cybermetrics, web science, web, Internet, quantitative methods, scientometrics, bibliometrics

Contents

1. **Introduction** 1
    1.1 New Problems: Web-Based Phenomena 1
    1.2 Old Problems: Offline Phenomena Reflected Online 3
    1.3 History and Definition 5
    1.4 Book Overview 6

2. **Web Impact Assessment** 9
    2.1 Web Impact Assessment Via Web Mentions 11
    2.2 Bespoke Web Citation Indexes 14
    2.3 Content Analysis 17
        2.3.1 Category Choices 17
        2.3.2 Sampling Methods 18
        2.3.3 Example 19
        2.3.4 Validity 20
    2.4 URL Analysis of the Spread of Results 21
    2.5 Web Impact Reports 23
    2.6 Web Citation Analysis—An Information Science Application 24
    2.7 Advanced Web Impact Studies 26
    2.8 Summary 26

3. **Link Analysis** 27
    3.1 Background: Link Counts as a Type of Information 27
    3.2 Types of Webometric Link Analysis 28
    3.3 Link Impact Assessments 29
        3.3.1 Interpreting the Results 31
        3.3.2 Alternative Link Counting Methods 32
        3.3.3 Case Study: Links to ZigZagMag.com 32
    3.4 Content Analysis of Links 33
    3.5 Link Relationship Mapping 35
        3.5.1 Case Studies 38

3.6   Colink Relationship Mapping 41

3.7   Link Impact Reports 44

3.8   Large-Scale Link Analysis with Multiple Site Groups 44

3.9   Link Differences Between Sectors—An Information Science Application 45

3.10   Summary 46

4.   **Blog Searching** 47

4.1   Blog Search Engines 47

4.2   Date-Specific Searches 48

4.3   Trend Detection 49

4.4   Checking Trend Detection Results 52

4.5   Limitations of Blog Data 54

4.6   Advanced Blog Analysis Techniques 55

4.7   Summary 56

5.   **Automatic Search Engine Searches: LexiURL Searcher** 57

5.1   Introduction to LexiURL Searcher 58

5.2   LexiURL Searcher Web Impact Reports 58

        5.2.1   Web Impact Reports—Classic Interface Example 61

5.3   LexiURL Searcher Link Impact Reports 64

        5.3.1   Link Impact Reports—Classic Interface Example 64

5.4   LexiURL Searcher for Network Diagrams 65

        5.4.1   Rearranging, Saving, and Printing Network Diagrams 65

        5.4.2   Network Diagram—Classic Interface Example 67

        5.4.3   Colink Network Diagrams 68

5.5   LexiURL Searcher Additional Features 69

6.   **Web Crawling: SocSciBot** 71

6.1   Web Crawlers 71

6.2   Overview of SocSciBot 73

6.3   Network Diagrams of Sets of Web Sites with SocSciBot 73

6.4   Other Uses for Web Crawls 78

7.   **Search Engines and Data Reliability** 81

7.1   Search Engine Architecture 81

        7.1.1   Duplicate and Near-Duplicate Elimination 83

7.2   Comparing Different Search Engines 84

7.3   Research Into Search Engine Results 84

7.4   Modeling the Web's Link Structure 86

8.   **Tracking User Actions Online**... 89
    8.1   Single-Site Web Analytics and Log File Analysis... 89
    8.2   Multiple-Site Web Analytics.. 91
    8.3   Search Engine Log File Analysis 91

9.   **Advanced Techniques**... 93
    9.1   Query Splitting.. 93
    9.2   Virtual Memetics... 95
    9.3   Web Issue Analysis 96
    9.4   Data Mining Social Network Sites... 97
    9.5   Social Network Analysis and Small Worlds 99
    9.6   Folksonomy Tagging.. 100
    9.7   API Programming and Mashups.. 100

10.   **Summary and Future Directions** 103

Glossary 105

References 107

Author Biography 115

CHAPTER 1

Introduction

Webometrics is concerned with measuring aspects of the web: web sites, web pages, parts of web pages, words in web pages, hyperlinks, web search engine results. The importance of the web itself as a communication medium and for hosting an increasingly wide array of documents, from journal articles to holiday brochures, needs no introduction. Given this huge and easily accessible source of information, there are limitless possibilities for measuring or counting on a huge scale (e.g., the number of web sites, the number of web pages, the number of blogs) or on a smaller scale (e.g., the number of web sites in Ireland, the number of web pages in the CNN web site, the number of blogs mentioning Barack Obama before the 2008 presidential campaign). This book argues that it can be useful for social scientists to measure aspects of the web and explains how this can be achieved on both a small and large scale. The book is aimed at social scientists with research topics that are wholly or partly online (e.g., social networks, news, political communication) and social scientists with offline research topics with an online reflection, even if this is not a core component (e.g., diaspora communities, consumer culture, linguistic change). The book is also aimed at library and information science students in the belief that the knowledge and techniques described will be useful for them to guide and aid other social scientists in their research. In addition, the techniques and issues are all directly relevant to library and information science research problems.

1.1   NEW PROBLEMS: WEB-BASED PHENOMENA

The clearest need for webometrics is to support research into web phenomena. For example, somebody studying the evolution of university web sites may wish to measure their growth in size over the past 10 years or the spread of specific technologies (e.g., JavaScript) in university web sites. Similarly, an investigation into the use of the web for political advocacy may involve measuring the sizes of relevant web sites, the pattern of hyperlinking between them, and the frequency of certain key concepts in them (e.g., poverty, the environment). In a project studying the web or part of the web, the researchers may choose purely qualitative techniques, purely quantitative techniques (e.g., webometrics), or a combination of both. The use of both qualitative and quantitative techniques is recommended as a general rule. Whereas qualitative techniques alone risk missing the big picture due to their necessarily small-scale nature, quantitative techniques risk being superficial or misleading if they are not complemented by supporting qualitative analysis. As a result, and where possible, this book introduces content analysis in parallel with purely quantitative web data collection. The content analysis component is especially important to help interpret quantitative data if more in-depth qualitative methods are not used.

The range of online problems that may benefit from a webometric analysis is vast because of the wide range of uses of the web itself. The following list illustrates various relevant issues and potential metrics.

- *Election web sites.* Political scientists or communication researchers may wish to know how official party web sites are used during election campaigns, perhaps seeking to identify key differences and commonalities between parties (Foot & Schneider, 2006). The results of such research can improve understanding of the political communication process and perhaps identifying factors leading to the success or failure of particular sites. One interesting but unsurprising finding is that political hyperlinking tends to occur between likeminded sites, suggesting that its main purpose is not to support substantive debate (Foot, Schneider, Dougherty, Xenos, & Larsen, 2003).

- *Online academic communication.* Information scientists, sociologists of science, and others may wish to analyze the changes in academic research processes and outcomes that have been triggered by the web. For example, one project ("The World Wide Web of Science" at the Oxford Internet Institute) investigated whether the web had led to a "winner takes all" situation in which the most successful researchers had become disproportionately more successful. Other studies have looked at patterns of interlinking between university, departmental, or research group web sites to explore issues such as the role of geography, discipline, and research productivity in hyperlinking (Barjak & Thelwall, 2008; Li, Thelwall, Wilkinson, & Musgrove, 2005; Thelwall, 2002a; Thelwall & Harries, 2004). One outcome of such research is that the number of links between academic web sites is influenced by the geographic distance between them as well as geopolitical and linguistic factors.

- *Bloggers as amateur journalists.* Media and journalism researchers have displayed interest in the role of bloggers in news production, especially as a source of new stories. This has been triggered by a few high-profile cases, such as outrage at a speech of U.S. senator Lott by a blogger, which eventually became a major news story and led to his resignation. As a result of the interest in blog-sourced news stories, quantitative measures, such as the number of hyperlinks from mainstream media sites to bloggers, have become relevant to shed some light on the extent of this (acknowledged) connection (e.g., Adamic & Glance, 2005).

- *Social networking*. Communication, media, sociology, and other researchers have recognized the significance of social network sites such as Facebook and MySpace because of their spectacular success, especially among youth, since the mid-2000s. Most research has understandably been primarily qualitative, particularly investigating broadly cultural issues, such as how young members conceptualize social network friendship and how they embed particular sites within their lives (boyd & Ellison, 2007). Some investigations have used quantitative methods, however, including to investigate the similarity between members expressed tastes and those of their friends (Liu, 2007) and the geographic spread of online friends (Escher, 2007).

To reiterate the key point, in all of the above examples, the phenomenon under study is new and web-based. In only one case (social networking) is the phenomenon essentially a specific technology, however. In two other examples, it includes a technology and a specific use: web sites for elections; blogs for amateur journalism. The example of online academic communication is more general because it involves many technologies including blogs, web sites, and digital libraries. The next section discusses research topics that are not new and unique to the web but are primarily offline issues that have an aspect or reflection on the web that can be usefully investigated.

1.2   OLD PROBLEMS: OFFLINE PHENOMENA REFLECTED ONLINE

Many issues are now investigated using the web that were previously investigated differently or were not investigated because it was impossible to do so. One activity that may be particularly changed is lexicography: the construction of dictionaries. Whereas previously, lexicographers would have to rely on intuition or the availability of relatively narrow or old data sources (e.g., the British National Corpus, Newswire data) to decide whether a new word was common enough to be added to a dictionary and what its meanings and uses are, the web provides a free data source for this. A simple web search for a word can give an indication of its popularity through the number of occurrences found and can give a set of examples of use from a wide range of online contexts, including the relatively informal language of blogs and MySpace. To emphasize the key point here, lexicographers are not primarily interested in online language, but the web is nevertheless a useful data source for its ability to reflect offline language and language changes. Of course, online language is important too, even for lexicographers, but it is somewhat peripheral to their main task.

The following list contains a selection of "old" problems on which webometric approaches can shed new light.

- *The impact or spread of ideas*. Many organizations have the goal of spreading a set of ideas. For example, advocacy groups may wish to raise awareness of environmental issues, poverty, health concerns, or the plight of prisoners of conscience. In addition, government-funded bodies may be tasked with spreading information about concepts deemed economically beneficial, such as the need for innovation in business and local government services, healthy eating practices, or the need for advance catastrophe avoidance planning. Similarly, advertisers may be tasked with raising brand awareness for a business or creating a positive association with a product. Some of these idea-based activities have tangible, measurable outcomes, such as product sales, or could be measured with traditional opinion-gathering techniques such as questionnaires, but for other activities, this is not an option or is impractical. The advantages of the web for gaining evidence of the spread of ideas, for example, by counting the number of web pages or blogs mentioning a key phrase, are that the data are easily accessible via search engines, large-scale coverage is possible, and the data collection process is passive and relatively cheap. There are important disadvantages too, such as a lack of control over the web "sample" used and the restriction to web-only data. In summary, the web can often be used for quick, indicative results and, in some cases, can be used for more in-depth studies.

- *Public opinion.* Governments often need to be aware of public opinion about topics such as immigration, genetically modified crops, and education policies. Moreover, companies would typically like to know consumer reactions to their products and services in as much detail as possible. Although traditional market research techniques such as questionnaires or focus groups address these needs, web-based data could be a more regular, timelier, and cheaper source. In addition, the web can be a preferred source if the phenomenon investigated is online, such as blogger reactions to a new computer game release. For some types of question, the web is in fact the only possible source. In particular, to discover how public opinion has changed over time regarding a topic previously not investigated, the web's function as a de facto archive of old web pages (in addition to the Internet Archive itself) is a unique source.

- *Informal scholarly communication.* The research process is extensively studied by scientometricians both to identify and reward successful researchers and to understand research processes to help researchers become more efficient or to inform doctoral training. Before the web, the latter type of investigation was much more difficult than the former. Successful research can be identified by offline means such as citation analysis, peer review, and funding calculations (Geisler, 2000; Moed, 2005a). The processes of research are typically unpublished, however, including informal chats between investigators, talks at conferences, and the formation of research teams. Although research processes have been studied before the web by sociologists of science (e.g., Latour & Woolgar, 1979) and information scientists (Crane, 1972), the investigations have tended to be very time-consuming and small-scale to gather sufficient data (e.g., by watching researchers at work or interviewing conference attendees). The web has made investigations of research processes possible on a larger scale because much informal scholarly communication now occurs on-line or leaves a trace online. For example, conference proceedings are often posted on the web, research groups tend to have informative web sites, and academic debates can occur in blogs or discussion lists with web-based archives. One study (the RESCAR project) took advantage of research group web sites to investigate just one aspect: researcher mobility. Another compared web-based and traditional bibliometric methods (Author Cocitation Analysis) for mapping the structure of academic fields (Zuccala, 2006).

Following the above introduction to webometrics and examples of the old and new problems to which it may be applied, this chapter concludes with a definition of webometrics, a history of its origins, and a brief introduction to webometric methods.

1.3   HISTORY AND DEFINITION

The term *webometrics* was coined in print by an article by Almind and Ingwersen (1997), which identified the web as an important source for measuring documents and information. Shortly after this, information scientists recognized that many powerful web measurements could be conducted using the new powerful advanced search features of one of the top search engines of the day: Alta-Vista (Ingwersen, 1998; Rodríguez i Gairín, 1997). In particular, AltaVista's link search capabilities provided large-scale link measurements to be conducted for the first time. This was illustrated in a study that included a count of the number of web pages in each Scandinavian country that linked to the pages of each other Scandinavian country (Ingwersen, 1998).

The ability to research web links using AltaVista proved particularly influential in triggering webometric research. This was because hyperlinks are structurally similar to academic citations in the sense that they point from a source document to a target document. Academic citations have been used for many years before the web by those wishing to track or assess the impact of research (Borgman & Furner, 2002; Garfield, 1970; Moed, 2005a; Nicolaisen, 2007). The similarity of links and citations, together with universities being early adopters of the web, resulted in the emergence of a number of important natural research goals. These attempted to assess whether hyperlinks could be used in similar ways to academic citations, the validity of using link counts and AltaVista data in research, and the best ways of counting links (e.g., Thelwall, 2001b). In parallel with this link analysis strand, other information scientists investigated the reliability and coverage of search engines and changes in the content of the web or individual collections of web pages (Bar-Ilan, 2004). These three types of web-based measurement research came to be collectively known as webometrics.

The term *cybermetrics* arose in parallel with the development of webometrics. This term was used to describe essentially the same research as webometrics and was the name of an electronic journal launched in 1997 and a series of workshops attached primarily to the biannual conference of the International Society for Scientometrics and Informetrics starting in 1996. The term *cybermetrics* was particularly preferred in Spain, where the word webometrics has an unimpressive popular connotation ("egg/testicle measurer"). The difference between the two terms was resolved by allowing cybermetrics to be more general—referring to non-web Internet research, such as email or newsgroup studies, in addition to web research (Björneborn & Ingwersen, 2004).

Long after its creation, webometrics was given its accepted definition as "the study of web-based phenomena using quantitative techniques and drawing upon informetric methods" (Björneborn & Ingwersen, 2004). The importance of this definition was its inclusion of informetric methods as a defining characteristic, placing webometrics as a purely information science field. *Informetrics* is a term used within information science to refer to quantitative research centered on measuring information. This includes citation analysis, for example. The definition thus excludes non-information science research based on web measuring, such as computer science attempts to measure the size of the web (Lawrence & Giles, 1999) and statistical physics searches for mathematical laws of linking (Barabási & Albert, 1999), although in both these cases, similarities could be drawn with prior informetric research (e.g., Ding & Marchionini, 1996; Rousseau, 1997).

In this book, its informetric heritage is downplayed and webometrics is defined in a method-centered manner as "the study of web-based content with primarily quantitative methods for social science research goals using techniques that are not specific to one field of study." The purpose of this definition is to set webometrics free from informetrics and aim it at a wide social science audience while excluding field-specific methods such as linguistic analyses of online language. The restriction to social science goals also excludes purely mathematical analyses of web-based content. Note also that although early webometrics research explicitly analyzed the web as a document network, the above definition does not rule out analyses of web page contents. Finally, the definition is broad enough to encompass research by people who would not describe themselves as webometricians but as researchers using web measurements in other fields.

1.4 BOOK OVERVIEW

This book focuses on three main webometric techniques: web impact assessment, link analysis, and blog searching. These are each dealt with in a separate chapter that describes when they can be applied, issues that arise when they are used, and their main variations. An important part of this book is the introduction of practical software to carry out the main techniques described. In the case of blog searching, this software is free online in the form of blog search web sites such as blogpulse.

com. For web impact assessment and link analysis, two programs are introduced, each in a separate chapter. The first, LexiURL Searcher (free at lexiurl.wlv.ac.uk) can automatically construct network diagrams and reports based on data extracted from commercial search engine results. The second program, SocSciBot 4 (free at socscibot.wlv.ac.uk) can also construct network diagrams and reports but gathers its data from crawls of sets of web sites or lists of web pages. The use of these programs is explained in this book to equip readers with the ability to conduct webometric studies with the minimum of hassle.

Although Chapters 2 to 6 give the necessary information to carry out a set of core webometric techniques, some additional information about the web and web users is needed to help interpret investigation results. Chapter 7 partly fills this gap by discussing search engines and web crawlers, particularly focussing on the reliability of their results. In addition, Chapter 8 introduces several methods to count or track the actions of web users.

Chapter 9 contains a set of issues and techniques that complement those introduced in the other chapters but which are not necessary for all projects or which are more specialized and less generally useful. This chapter does not contain the same level of detail as the others but references additional sources when necessary. The book concludes with a summary and a discussion of future research directions. Additional information is available at the book's web site webometrics.wlv .ac.uk.

Finally, please note that this book is arranged from theory to practice, but users with a practical orientation are encouraged to skip Chapters 2 and 3 initially and read any or all of Chapters 4 to 6 for practical information about how to collect and analyze data using blog search engines, such as SocSciBot and LexiURL Searcher. Please read Chapters 2 and 3 afterward, however, for important contextual information and theory.

• • • •

CHAPTER 2

Web Impact Assessment

Web impact assessment is the evaluation of the "web impact" of documents or ideas by counting how often they are mentioned online. The underpinning idea is that, other factors being equal, documents or ideas having more impact are likely to be mentioned online more. This concept essentially originates from an early study that counted how often prominent academics were mentioned online and the contexts in which they were mentioned (Cronin, Snyder, Rosenbaum, Martinson, & Callahan, 1998). The results were proposed as a new way of getting insights into "academic interaction."

Researchers that are interested in examining the impact of specific ideas or documents may therefore benefit from a web impact assessment. For instance, the goal may be to compare the influence, spread, or support of competing academic theories, political candidates, or a number of similar books. In such cases, comparing the web impact of the theories/candidates/books (e.g., the number of web pages mentioning each one) can be a proxy for their offline impact or a direct measure of web impact. Below are some examples.

- For academic theories, it would be interesting to find out in which countries and universities they are mentioned. Although it would be impractically difficult to find this out offline (e.g., via phone calls or interviews with random academics across the globe), it would be much easier to do this online by counting web mentions using the webometric techniques described in this chapter. This would give useful results, but of course the absence of a theory from a university web site would not always mean that the theory was unknown in the university. It might be known and even taught but not mentioned online. Hence, the web results would be indicative of a minimum level of awareness rather than definitive. Nevertheless, in a comparative study of two or more theories, each one would suffer from the same limitations and so comparing the results between them should be informative about which was the best known overall.
- For the example of two (or more) political candidates, the ultimate indicator of success would be the votes polled. A web impact assessment would be useful to evaluate the online component of the candidates' campaigns, however. This could judge how successful each

campaign was as well as where it was successful, with whom, and why. For such an issue, the restriction of the data collected to just online information would be an advantage rather than a limitation. A web impact assessment could also be used beforehand to help judge the relative success of their campaigns or even to predict a winner, but opinion polls would be better for both of these tasks.

- To compare the sphere of influence of two books, web searches could be conducted to identify how often each one was mentioned and in which countries. In this case, publishers' sales figures would give more accurate information about the geographic spread of purchasers but would not be able to give data on the context in which the books were read or the opinions of the purchasers. This gap could be filled by web searches finding information such as blog postings reviewing or discussing the books.

A related commercial application of web impact assessment is for organizations producing or promoting ideas or information and needing to be able to provide evidence of their spread or impact. For example, a public body charged with promoting innovation may need to provide evidence of the impact of its work. It may not be possible to directly measure the desired outcomes (e.g., business innovation) and so such an organization may be forced to turn to indirect indicators, such as the number of attendees at its events, its press coverage (via the LexisNexis database), or the number of requests for its literature. The Web provides a new way to generate indirect indicators of this kind. Web searches can be used to count the number of times that its publications or concepts have been mentioned online. A publication that has been mentioned frequently online, for example, in blogs, news web sites, and online reports, is likely to have had a big impact. Moreover, an analysis of web impact could be conducted comparatively, with mentions of the reports or ideas of similar organizations also measured to benchmark performance.

The practice of evaluating the impact of documents through counting how often they are mentioned predates the web in the form of citation analysis (Borgman & Furner, 2002; Garfield, 1970; Moed, 2005a; Nicolaisen, 2007), but the principles are very similar. In citation analysis, the number of times an academic article is cited by another article (e.g., included in a reference list) is taken as an indicator of the impact of the research described in it. The basis for this, drawing on Merton's (1973) sociology of science, is that science is a cumulative process and that articles which get cited by other articles are likely to be demonstrating their contribution to the overall scientific endeavour. Numerous scientists around the world are now assessed partly based on how many citations their published articles attract. Web impact assessment cannot claim the same deep theoretical foundations as citation analysis and the evidence provided by online mentions is consequently less strong, but it can nevertheless give useful web impact indicators. The following sections give advice about conducting a web impact assessment based on mentions in general web documents, and other sections discuss the subtopic of web citation analysis.

2.1   WEB IMPACT ASSESSMENT VIA WEB MENTIONS

A simple type of web impact assessment is to take a collection of ideas or documents and then submit them as phrase searches into a commercial search engine, using the reported hit count estimates as the impact evidence. The hit count estimates are the numbers reported by search engines in their results pages as the estimated maximum number of matching pages (e.g., the figure 373,000,000 in "Results 1–10 of about 373,000,000 for Obama" at the top of a Google search results page). If a comparative assessment is needed for benchmarking purposes, then the same procedure should be repeated for an additional collection of ideas or documents chosen from a suitable similar source. Table 2.1 gives a simple example of a comparison of the web impact of four medieval history books.

The simple procedure above has a number of drawbacks, but some refinements can be used to make the evidence more robust. The first refinement is that the keyword searches should be checked to ensure that the overwhelming majority (e.g., 90%) of the pages returned correctly mention the desired document or idea. It is likely that some of the searches will return many spurious matches, especially if they are short or use common words. In these cases the search should be modified to filter out false matches. For example, in the case of a book, the author could be added to the search (as in Table 2.1). In the case of an idea, words very commonly associated with it could be added. Unfortunately, modifying the keyword searches makes subsequent comparisons unfair, but there may be no alternatives and so any unfairness of this nature should be reported alongside the results.

TABLE 2.1: A comparative web impact assessment of four books.		
BOOK TITLE	**GOOGLE QUERY USED (TITLE AND AUTHOR)**	**HIT COUNT ESTIMATE**
Handbook of Medieval Sexuality	"Handbook of Medieval Sexuality" Bullough	3,780
The End of the House of Lancaster	"The End of the House of Lancaster" Storey	2,610
The Reign of King Henry VI	"The Reign of King Henry VI" Griffiths	1,340
Medieval Women: A Social History of Women in England 450–1500	"Medieval Women: A Social History of Women in England 450–1500" Leyser	973

For some searches it may be impossible to modify them in any way to get mainly correct matches, and these can either be dropped from the analysis or their results manually checked to identify correct matches. An example of the latter situation is the physics journal *Small*: it is impossible to construct a web search with reasonable coverage such that the majority of matching pages mention this journal because its title is such a common word.

A second refinement is that it is best to identify and count all matching pages rather than rely on search engine hit count estimates. This is because these estimates can sometimes be unreliable—typically they overestimate the number of results that the search engines would return. It is not always possible to count all matches because search engines report a maximum of 1,000. This technique is therefore only practical for searches that generate fewer total matches. There is an alternative, however, which is discussed later in the book: to automate the URL counting and to use the "query splitting" technique to get additional matches when the maximum of 1,000 is reached. Table 2.2 contains web pages counted via their URLs in the results pages for the specified Google search. Note that all the results are significantly smaller than the estimates reported in Table 2.1.

A third refinement is to count matching web sites rather than matching web *pages* (i.e., URLs). This is important because some web sites may mention an idea repeatedly, whereas others may mention it only once. Although repeated mentions probably suggest more interest in the idea than a single mention, it could also just mean that similar content has been copied across multiple pages in a site. Hence, it seems safest to count mentioning web sites rather than web pages.

TABLE 2.2: A comparative web impact assessment of four books—improved figures.		
BOOK TITLE	**GOOGLE QUERY USED (TITLE AND AUTHOR)**	**URLs**
Handbook of Medieval Sexuality	"Handbook of Medieval Sexuality" Bullough	782
The End of the House of Lancaster	"The End of the House of Lancaster" Storey	653
The Reign of King Henry VI	"The Reign of King Henry VI" Griffiths	541
Medieval Women: A Social History of Women in England 450–1500	"Medieval Women: A Social History of Women in England 450-1500" Leyser	498

Although there is no single accepted definition of "web site," it is convenient and reasonable to equate web sites with domain names so that two pages sharing the same domain name are always deemed to come from the same site. As with URL counting, this process can be automated (e.g., using LexiURL Searcher), as discussed in other chapters in this book. Table 2.3 contains web pages counted by first extracting their URLs from the results pages for the specified Google search, then identifying the domain name for each URL, then counting the number of unique domain names in the resulting list.

Even with the above refinements, there are disadvantages with web impact measurements. The principal disadvantage is that the unregulated and anarchic nature of the web means that the scope of the web sample is likely to be unclear. For example, suppose that an idea of "Farm Widgets" is important to the organization PromoteBusinessWidgets. Farm Widgets are likely to be mentioned by PromoteBusinessWidgets in its web site (and hence picked up in a web impact report) if PromoteBusinessWidgets has a web site and if that web site is sufficiently informative to mention the importance of the idea. This seems more likely to be the case if PromoteBusinessWidgets is a large organization or if it is an organization that regards its web site as important. As a result of cases like this, it is possible for an idea or publication to have a (small) web impact even when it is not

TABLE 2.3: A comparative web impact assessment of four books—counted by web site, based on the full domain names of URLs matching the Google query.

BOOK TITLE	GOOGLE QUERY USED (TITLE AND AUTHOR)	WEB SITES
Handbook of Medieval Sexuality	"Handbook of Medieval Sexuality" Bullough	401
The End of the House of Lancaster	"The End of the House of Lancaster" Storey	378
The Reign of King Henry VI	"The Reign of King Henry VI" Griffiths	327
Medieval Women: A Social History of Women in England 450–1500	"Medieval Women: A Social History of Women in England 450–1500" Leyser	288

well known outside the originating organization. This impact could be multiplied if the organization maintained several web sites or placed adverts online. Conversely, a document could be widely read by a community that does not extensively blog or publish online. For example, a leaflet with guidelines for the safe use of Zimmer frames would presumably be targeted at the elderly who seem to be a sector of society that does not extensively publish online. As a result of factors like these, web impact evidence should be interpreted as indicative rather than definitive. Web impact evidence would be strongest in cases where it would be reasonable to assume that web impact would fairly reflect offline impact or for cases where a web-based phenomenon is being assessed (e.g., blogging or online electioneering).

The following are guidelines for an initial web impact assessment. All the necessary raw data for this are provided by LexiURL Searcher reports using a set of relevant queries (see Chapter 5).

- Compare the overall hit counts to discover which documents or ideas have the most impact, notice any particularly weak or strong performers, and comment on why they might be weak or strong.
- Identify the most popular types of site for each document or idea (e.g., news, blogs, universities) and comment on why they might be popular.
- Identify differences in the most popular types of site between the different documents or ideas and comment on why the differences might be there. Are any of the differences surprising or glaring omissions? For instance, an academic document not attracting mentions from any universities would be unusual.
- Identify the most popular countries for each document or idea [e.g., from the top-level domains (TLDs) of the results, ignoring .com, .net, .org] and comment on why they might be mentioned so often in these countries.
- Identify differences in the most popular countries between the different documents or ideas and comment on why the differences might be there. Are any of the differences surprising or glaring omissions? For example, perhaps one document has attracted a lot of attention in China or another document is the only one not mentioned in Spain.

2.2 BESPOKE WEB CITATION INDEXES

An impact assessment exercise may less concerned with general web mentions of an idea or report than with mentions in online academic documents or other formal reports. In such cases, general web searches would likely produce too many spurious matches to be useful. It is relatively easy to narrow down the general web search results, however, using the knowledge that academic articles and reports are normally in PDF format when posted online, although they may sometimes be posted as Word documents or in other word processing formats. As a result, most of mentioning documents can probably be found by running an appropriate keyword search but turning it into an advanced search by restricting the results to only PDFs, for example, by adding the advanced search command `filetype:pdf` to the search. To include Word documents in the results, additional searches can be run with `filetype:doc` or `filetype:docx` to capture Word documents. The number of matching documents could then be counted and used as the impact evidence, as in Table 2.4. Totalling the hit count estimates in Table 2.4 gives an overall report impact estimate as follows.

1. Ready steady innovate!: 3 + 0 = 3
2. Agricultural widgets in Norfolk: 1 + 1 = 2
3. Innovative agricultural widget designs: 0 + 0 = 0

Searches restricted to a single document type, as above, typically generate many fewer results than generic searches. This often gives scope for additional human processing to filter, check, and add extra value in the form of context checking. If accurate results are important, then the results should

TABLE 2.4: A comparative web impact assessment of three reports based on the number of citing PDF or Word documents found.

REPORT TITLE (MADE UP)	GOOGLE QUERY USED	HIT COUNT ESTIMATE
Ready steady innovate!	"Ready steady innovate" filetype:pdf	3
Agricultural widgets in Norfolk	"Agricultural widgets in Norfolk" filetype:pdf	1
Innovative agricultural widget designs	"Innovative agricultural widget designs" filetype:pdf	0
Ready steady innovate!	"Ready steady innovate" filetype:doc	0
Agricultural widgets in Norfolk	"Agricultural widgets in Norfolk" filetype:doc	1
Innovative agricultural widget designs	"Innovative agricultural widget designs" filetype:doc	0

be filtered to remove spurious matches and duplicate documents. Spurious matches—results matching the search but not mentioning the desired document—should always be checked for, of course. Duplicates are possible because reports may be circulated and reposted in different places online by readers, if permission is granted to do so. Also, there may be PDF and Word versions of the same document. In a large set of results, duplicates can be identified by listing the titles of the identified documents and using the titles to suggest duplicates (e.g., by sorting alphabetically by title to place common titles together for easier identification).

In addition to general search engines, specialist search services such as Google Scholar may also be able to reveal additional online (and even offline) citing documents (Jascó, 2005; Mayr & Walter, 2007; Vaughan & Shaw, 2008). In some cases, it is also possible to search directly for citations in these specialist search services if they contain their own citation index.

Significant extra contextual information can be generated from the search results by building a bespoke web citation index. A web citation index is simply a list of the titles and types of each correctly identified citing document, as shown in Table 2.5. This can be built by visiting all the results

TABLE 2.5: A web citation index from human evaluations of the search results, as produced in Table 2.4.

CITING REPORT TITLE	CITING REPORT TYPE	CITED REPORT
Regional Improvement and Efficiency Strategy for Yorkshire (PDF)	Research report	Ready steady innovate!
U.K. parliamentary agricultural select committee report, September 2008 (PDF)	Research report	Ready steady innovate!
We know what to do but we don't always do it (PDF)	Conference paper	Ready steady innovate!
Assessment of the effectiveness of rural development schemes (MS Word)	Research report	Agricultural widgets in Norfolk
England's rural areas: steps to release their economic potential (PDF)	Research report	Agricultural widgets in Norfolk

obtained as in Table 2.4 and extracting the document titles and identifying the document types. This index succinctly summarizes the contexts in which the reports have been found useful. Note that duplicate elimination can be conducted at the same time as building the web citation index. If necessary, additional columns could be added reporting more information about why each report was cited, but this is more of a content analysis, as described in the following section. Although there are many citation indexes on the web already as part of services such as Google Scholar, the purpose of the bespoke index is to summarize relevant information for one particular purpose rather than to generate a widely used searchable resource.

2.3   CONTENT ANALYSIS

It can be difficult to interpret or explain the significance of the statistics in a web impact assessment. This is because the variety of reasons why a web page could be created, including negative reasons like spam marketing, make it difficult to give a simple explanation of what a count of online mentions really means. This gap can be filled by finding out what types of web pages are common in the results to give a general description of what the statistics represent. In consequence, qualitative investigations should always be conducted as part of any web impact assessment, except perhaps when a bespoke web citation index is the primary output and the clients wish to read the documents in the citation index. Qualitative information about the web citations can be obtained by visiting a random sample of web pages from the study (i.e., pages matching the keyword searches) and reading them to find out what they are about and the context in which the keywords were mentioned. This is best formalized as a content analysis.

A web impact content analysis is a systematic categorization of a set of search results based on human inspection of the contents of the matching URLs. The end result is a set of categories and an estimate for the number of search results fitting each category. The categories themselves can be predetermined, perhaps from categories previously used in a similar exercise, but it is best if the categorization scheme is implemented flexibly so that it can be expanded if pages appear that do not fit the existing categories well. The object of such an expansion should always be to give additional relevant information about the context of the citations. It is also possible to use an inductive content analysis: starting with no categories at all but grouping similar documents together to start with and then later formalizing this into defined categories. This approach is recommended for new types of web impact exercises.

2.3.1   Category Choices

The choice of categories for the content analysis should be related to the objective of the web impact assessment. Although it is possible to classify web pages in many different ways (e.g., visual attractiveness, colour scheme, national origins, owning organization size, main topic, industrial sector, embedded technologies), the categories should primarily be chosen to inform the web impact exercise. In particular, it is likely that the categories will address who created the citing pages or the purpose of the citing pages. When the content analysis is complete, it should be used to complete sentences like: "Document/idea X was mainly mentioned online by A and B" or "Document/idea X was mainly mentioned online because of A and B." If the primary topic of interest is the organizational origins of the online citations, then it is likely that many classifications would include categories for the main organizations represented (e.g., universities, the press, companies, government) as well as a category for individuals (e.g., bloggers, personal home pages, social network profiles). If the primary topic of interest is the citation types, then the categories could encompass common document types (e.g., press stories, academic papers, blog postings) or common topics (e.g., business information, recreational information, geographic information).

The categorization process can either be informal or formal. A formal categorization should use a recognized content analysis method (e.g., Neuendorf, 2002), and this is recommended for research to be published in academic outlets. Formal content analysis can be time-consuming, however, because it involves extra states to ensure of the validity of the results, such as cross-checking between multiple coders and the use of a formal coding scheme. An informal content analysis, which could be done by one person using intuitive judgments of categories, is appropriate for pilot studies or for situations where a high degree of validity of the results is not essential.

2.3.2   Sampling Methods

In theory, a content analysis could include a classification of all pages matching the keyword searches. Nevertheless, this comprehensive approach is often likely to be impractical because there are too many pages to classify in the time available. In such cases a sample of an equal number from each keyword search should be used. If possible, this sample should be selected at random from the URLs or sites (depending on which are being counted; see above) matching each search using a random number generator. A rough-and-ready simple alternative would be to use a systematic sample instead, however. For example, if there are 200 matches for a keyword search and the sample for the content analysis has been selected as 10, then starting at the 10th match and taking every 20th result from then on would give a good spread of results and seems unlikely to introduce a systematic bias.

How many sites should be classified if a sampling approach is being used? This is a difficult issue because classification is quite time-consuming, and for robust results, a large number of pages must be classified. This is particularly true if it is important to distinguish between the proportions in categories for the different keyword searches. In most cases, however, it is sufficient to give an overall approximate proportion of web pages in each category because the purpose of the classification is to inform the analysis of the results rather than to identify statistically significant differences between categories. For a quick investigation, such as for a pilot study, as few as 30 classified pages could be sufficient, although 100 is recommended as the normal minimum number. If it is important to distinguish the proportions in categories between different keyword searches, then a larger sample size is likely to be needed and a formal approach should also be taken for the classification process itself. In this case, a standard text on content analysis is recommended to give guidelines on the classification process and the minimum number of classifications needed (e.g., Neuendorf, 2002).

2.3.3   Example

The case below illustrates the results of a classification exercise. It is taken from a web impact analysis for publications produced by the U.K. National Endowment for Science, Technology and the Arts (NESTA) in 2006 to 2007. After extracting a list of web sites mentioning each publication, a random sample of 324 web pages was classified (a maximum of one per web site) and the results are shown below. The classification was created inductively, primarily focusing on the type of organization mentioning the documents. The scheme below was adopted and the results are in Figure 2.1.

- Academic—university or other similar academic institution, including research-only government and nonprofit research institutes.
- Press or blogs—online newspapers and online versions of offline newspapers, unless the newspaper is specific to a company or affiliated to an academic organization (e.g., a regional research forum). Includes all blogs, whether written by journalists, professionals, or the general public.
- Industry—commercial organizations.
- Government—government departments and government-funded organizations.

The categories in Figure 2.1 were chosen to reveal the organizational sectors that mentioned NESTA publications so that the organization could understand and develop its audience reach. As a result of Figure 2.1, the web impact statistics for the NESTA reports can be interpreted primarily as evidence of government and press/blogger interest and should not be interpreted as evidence of commercial interest. This is something that would not be obvious without a content analysis.

Note that if the main web impact report statistics for a study are reported based on counting web sites rather than web pages, then the classification sample should be randomly selected based

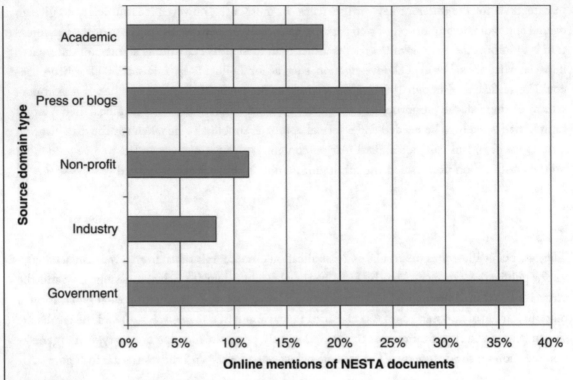

FIGURE 2.1: Sources of mentions of NESTA publications (324 classified).

on web sites with a maximum of one page classified per site. This was the case for Figure 2.1: a maximum of one web page per site was classified. The random selection of pages on a per-site basis can be awkward, but if LexiURL Searcher is used for data collection, then appropriate random lists are automatically produced as part of its output (see Chapter 5, Automatic Search Engine Searches: LexiURL Searcher).

2.3.4 Validity

An important issue is the validity of the human judgments used to make the classifications. Most web impact assessments have used a single human classifier, and this seems appropriate in cases where the purpose of the classification is to give context to the results rather than to accurately distinguish between categories. Nevertheless, it is more reliable to have multiple classifiers using the same scheme and then to assess the extent to which their judgments agree. Information about levels of agreement can then be reported as evidence of the robustness of the classification results. If this level of classification accuracy is needed, then a standard content analysis textbook is recommended as a guide for the procedures involved (e.g., Neuendorf, 2002).

As the above discussion illustrates, whereas a simple "quick and dirty" content analysis can be straightforward, a robust and accurate classification is more complex and far more time-consuming, involving many more classifications and the use of multiple classifiers. If a classification is for a formal academic publication and distinguishing between categories is important, then the latter type will be necessary. If the classification is for an organization that does not need, or want to pay for, very accurate results, then a simpler exercise is likely to be sufficient. Similarly, students practicing the technique should start with a simple classification as the time involved with a larger one might not be justifiable.

2.4   URL ANALYSIS OF THE SPREAD OF RESULTS

URL analysis is the extraction of information from the URLs of the results returned by a search engine search for a web impact assessment. This takes advantage of the structure implicit in most URLs, such as the domain name of a URL tending to reflect the organization hosting the page.

When assessing the impact of documents or ideas online, it can be useful to identify where the impact comes from in geographic terms or which web sites host the most mentions. Geographic spread can be estimated to some extent by extracting the TLDs of the URLs or web sites matching the keyword searches. Most TLDs correspond directly to nations so that, for example, if 50% of the matches to a keyword search have .fr domains, then they probably originate in France. It is relatively easy to identify and count TLDs in a list of matching URLs or sites and so TLD statistics can be calculated relatively quickly, especially if the process is automated (e.g., by LexiURL Searcher). An important drawback, however, is the prevalence of generic TLDs, such as .com, which are not nation-specific. If accurate geographic statistics are needed, then a random sample of the generic TLD URLs or sites should be visited to identify their origins and the results used to predict the total number from each country represented.

Table 2.6 illustrates a table of TLDs extracted from a set of search engine results. The table confirms the anglophone bias that might be expected for a book about a medieval English King [United Kingdom, United States (edu), Canada, Australia (au), Ireland (ie)] but also contains a potential surprise in the form of six German web sites (de). No significance can be drawn from the .com, .org, .net, or .info results.

It can sometimes be useful to identify the sites that mention documents or ideas most frequently. This can be achieved by counting the number of pages represented for each web site in the results. Here, web sites can again be equated with full domain names. Although this information can be calculated manually in principle, it is easily automated with software such as LexiURL Searcher. Table 2.7 gives an example extracted from searches for web pages mentioning a particular Persian document. It shows that the site www.pendar.net mentioned the document most often and that many web sites mentioned the document frequently. If such a table is used, then the web sites

TABLE 2.6: TLDs of web sites matching the query: "The Reign of King Henry VI" Griffiths.

TLD	SITES	%
com	39	32.0
uk	25	20.5
edu	10	8.2
de, org	8	6.6
net	6	4.9
ca	4	3.3
info, nl, jp, es, au, ie, fr	2	1.6
ee, cn, pl, mx, nu, it, eu, at	1	0.8

TABLE 2.7: Web sites containing most pages mentioning a Persian document.

WEB SITE (DOMAIN NAME)	PAGES (URLS)	PERCENTAGE OF ALL URLS
www.pendar.net	114	10
www.dreamlandblog.com	100	9
www.ahmadnia.net	72	6
sibestaan.malakut.org	63	5
www.fasleno.com	55	5
noqte.com	52	5
www.mowlanayear.ir	39	3
www.khabgard.com	25	2

TABLE 2.8: Sites hosting most subdomains mentioning a Persian document.

HOSTING WEB SITE	SUBDOMAINS	PERCENTAGE OF ALL SUBDOMAINS
blogfa.com	84	18
blogspot.com	42	9
wordpress.com	19	4
blogsky.com	11	2
blogfa.ir	10	2
malakut.org	6	1
ketablog.com	5	1

should be visited to check that the document is not mentioned for a spurious reason, such as advertising. Note that some search engine results automatically restrict the number of matches per site to two per results page, and if this is the case, then the search engine option to disable site collapsing should be selected, if possible, to get the best results.

A similar summary is of the hosting web sites that contain the most (sub)domains mentioning the document or ideas from the queries used. This can be achieved automatically by equating the domain name endings with hosting web sites and counting the number of derivative domain names (subdomains). For example, blogs hosted by www.blogspot.com all have domain names ending with blogspot.com (e.g., webometrics.blogspot.com) and so counting the number of domain names ending in blogspot.com in the results reveals the number of blogspot blogs mentioning the documents or ideas from the original query. Table 2.8 illustrates the results from this kind of process for a search for a Persian document name. The table shows that the Persian blogging service blogfa.com hosts the most blogs mentioning the document but that several other blog services, including international sites such as wordpress.com and blogspot.com, also host blogs.

2.5   WEB IMPACT REPORTS

The previous sections decribe a range of separate web impact assessment techniques. Sometimes these methods can be used individually as part of a research project, but they can also be combined as

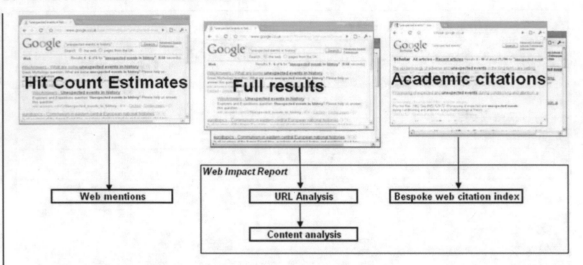

FIGURE 2.2: Types of web impact assessment.

part of a report into the web impact of a collection of documents or ideas. Figure 2.2 illutrates how three of the four techniques mentioned above can be combined into a web impact report that gives a rounded set of information. The web mentions are not included because the hit count estimate data are superseded by the URL analysis component. The web impact report is a recommended combination of types of information but may have to be customized for particular goals. For instance, there may not be an academic angle to the information and so the bespoke web citation index may not be needed. Similarly, for particular tasks, there may be additional relevant information, such as data about blog discussions, as introduced in Chapter 4 (Blog Searching), or about changes over time, as discussed in Section 9.2 (Virtual Memetics).

2.6 WEB CITATION ANALYSIS—AN INFORMATION SCIENCE APPLICATION

This section describes web impact assessment research addressing a specific type of problem within the academic discipline of information science. This example illustrates how web impact analyses can drive extensive academic research.

Web citation analysis is a type of web impact assessment that has been developed within the library and information science discipline. It typically involves web impact assessments using simple counts of web mentions for large collections of academic documents, such as journal articles, in conjunction with content analysis of the citations. The assessments tend not to use URL citation indexes because their purpose was theoretical and tend not to use URL analyses of the international spread of results because this is relatively unimportant for the research hypotheses.

Web citation analysis was pioneered by Vaughan and Shaw (2003) as an online compliment to traditional offline citation analysis. The latter focused on counting the number of times an article had been cited in other academic articles, for example, mentioned in reference lists. This figure is widely used as the indicator of the importance of an article (Moed, 2005a). Historically, (offline) citation analysis has mainly used databases of citations collated and maintained by the Institute for Scientific Information (ISI, now Thomson-Reuters). Previous authors had realized that search engines could be used to discover how often any article had been mentioned on the web but had applied this to whole journals rather than to individual articles (Smith, 1999).

Vaughan and Shaw (2003) used a new approach, extracting long lists of article titles from library and information science academic journals and comparing how often they were cited in ISI citation databases with how often they were cited on the web. They found that web citations were more numerous but correlated significantly with ISI citations and that just under half seemed to directly reflect scholarly or educational impact. As a result, web citations could be used as a replacement for ISI citations, including for journals not covered by the ISI. Nevertheless, there were disadvantages: some web citations were for relatively trivial reasons, such as online tables of contents for journals. In addition, constructing the searches was time-consuming. A follow-up study of biology, genetics, medicine, and multidisciplinary sciences gave similar results but a lower proportion of citations reflecting scholarly or intellectual impact (Vaughan & Shaw, 2005). A later study, of citations to the publications of library and information science faculty, found a smaller proportion of scholarly or educational impact citations, and almost 40% of the web citations came from lists of articles. It also confirmed that there were many more web citations per publication than citations recorded in the Web of Science academic citation databases. In contrast, Google Scholar citations almost exclusively reflected intellectual impact (92%) and were also more frequent than Web of Science citations, although less numerous than web citations (Vaughan & Shaw, 2008).

A number of other studies have also taken large samples of academic journal articles and evaluated the number of online citations to each, using a range of different techniques to identify citations. For example, one investigation coined the phrase "Google Web/URL citations" to encompass citations to either the title or the URL of an online article. In a comparison with Web of Science citations for open access journals in eight science and social science disciplines, the web citations were found to be relatively numerous and correlated with Web of Science citations in all disciplines except psychology. This study also confirmed that Google Scholar was a good source of citations, correlating significantly with Web of Science citations (Kousha & Thelwall, 2007).

In summary, a significant body of research has been developed that is concerned with using web impact analyses for the important but narrow task of developing methods to identify the online impact of academic journal articles. This shows the potential for web impact analyses to underpin research into specific online issues.

2.7   ADVANCED WEB IMPACT STUDIES

Advanced web impact studies are those that used additional techniques beyond those described above. One way that this can be achieved is by modifying the basic keyword searches used to reduce their scope. For instance, one study took a list of searches for 70,700 academic journal articles and modified them by adding the text `syllabus OR "reading list"` to derive searches designed to match online syllabuses. The purpose of the study was to assess the extent to which recent academic journal articles were mentioned in course syllabuses in a range of disciplines (Kousha & Thelwall, 2008). For this kind of web impact study, no content analysis is needed because the web pages matching the search are already tightly defined as academic syllabuses. The research found evidence that there were large disciplinary differences in the extent to which academic research was used in academic teaching. Such a conclusion would have taken much more time to reach using other methods such as questionnaires sent to a random sample of educators in various disciplines.

2.8   SUMMARY

Web impact analyses are based on counting and analyzing the URLs returned by search engines in response to queries designed to match documents or ideas. The purpose is to produce indicators of the extent to which the documents or ideas are mentioned online, either to directly assess web impact or to indirectly assess predominantly offline impact through measurement of the online component of that impact. Web impact assessment is relatively easy to conduct in a simple "quick and dirty" manner and in this form is useful to give a broad overview of the impact of a set of documents or ideas. Web impact analyses are more time-consuming to conduct in a robust manner because of the increased human effort involved in conducting high-quality content analyses. Content analysis is normally an important component of web impact analyses because of the need to interpret the figures produced. Content analysis is most needed for documents and ideas that have a broad appeal and least necessary for highly specialized documents or searches that are mentioned online in predictable specialized searches, as with the syllabus searches discussed above and probably with most academic publication web impact studies.

* * * *

CHAPTER 3

Link Analysis

Most webometric studies have been types of link analysis, using hyperlinks between web pages or web sites as the raw data. This chapter introduces a range of link analysis techniques and explains why links have attracted much interest.

3.1 BACKGROUND: LINK COUNTS AS A TYPE OF INFORMATION

Although hyperlinks are typically designed as a navigation aid, to help web users to jump quickly between web pages, they also contain implicit information that can be exploited for research purposes. A hyperlink can sometimes be regarded as an endorsement of the target page, especially if the creator of the link has chosen it to point to a useful or important page. For instance, hyperlinks in a course web site might all point to web sites with relevant high-quality information or to helpful resources such as online library catalogues. As a result of many links being created like this, it seems that the best and most useful pages tend to attract the most hyperlinks. For instance, the Google home page is linked to by at least a hundred million pages, and major news web sites can expect to attract at least a million links, whereas the average blog or personal home page could expect to attract few links or none at all because they are simply less useful.

The number of web pages linking to a given web page or web site is called its inlink count. The above discussion essentially argues that inlink counts may be a reasonable indicator of the importance of the target site or page. This property of inlink counts is exploited in Google's Page-Rank algorithm (Brin & Page, 1998), in Kleinberg's similar topic-based search algorithm HITS (Kleinberg, 1999), and also in the ranking algorithms of other search engines. These search ranking algorithms are designed so that the pages listed first in response to any standard keyword search tend to be those that attract the most links. If you query a search engine, then it will first identify pages that match your search and then list them in an order that its guesses will place the most useful ones first—using hyperlink counts as important evidence for this ordering.

Inlink counts are not a perfect source of evidence because not all hyperlinks are carefully created by web authors after consideration of which page would be the best link target. Many links between pages in a web site are created primarily for navigation within the site. As a result, these links are ignored or given low importance by search engines and are typically ignored in webometric link analyses. A different issue is that links are sometimes replicated within a web site. For example, a web site may have a link to Google on every page. It would not seem fair to count every such link because all are presumably the result of a single web author's decision to add a Google link everywhere. As a result, search engines and webometrics calculations often count a maximum of one link between any pair of web sites. In other words, pairs of linking web *sites* are counted rather than pairs of linking web *pages*. Here, a web site is normally either equated with the full domain name of each URL (e.g., www.microsoft.com, www.wlv.ac.uk, www.ucla.edu, www.bbc.co.uk) or with the ending of the URL associated with the domain name owner (e.g., microsoft.com, wlv.ac.uk, ucla.edu, bbc.co.uk).

In addition to links being useful indicators of the value of the target page, they often connect pages about the same topic and so are useful as indicators of content similarity (Chakrabarti, Joshi, Punera, & Pennock, 2002). Moreover, links can be created to reflect or acknowledge organizational connections. For example, a research group web site may link to the sites of other groups that it collaborates with, the organizations that have funded it, and to its parent university and department. Similarly, a local government body may link to its parent and subsidiary organizations' web sites and to companies that provide it with services. Finally, links are sometimes created for relatively trivial reasons, such as when an academic's home page contains links related to their hobbies. When carrying out a webometric link analysis, such links often form the unwanted "noise" in the results.

3.2   TYPES OF WEBOMETRIC LINK ANALYSIS

Partly reflecting the differing types of reason for creating links discussed above, there are two main types of webometric link analysis: link impact assessments and link relationship mappings. Link relationship mapping typically illustrates collections of web sites through the links associated with them. It includes link-based organizational relationship mapping and link-based maps of topic areas or organizations intended to reveal content similarity. In practice, these two types often overlap.

Link impact assessments typically start with a collection of web sites and compare the number of web pages or web sites that link to each one. This is similar to the web impact assessment using keyword searches discussed in the previous chapter. The purpose of link impact assessment is often to evaluate whether a given web site has a high link-based web impact compared to its peers. Link-based impact can also be used as an indirect indicator of other attributes of the owning organization. For example, one study has shown that links to U.K. universities correlate highly with their research productivity, suggesting that link impact might also be used as an estimator of research productivity for universities in countries that do not publish research evaluation results (Thelwall, 2001b). The well-known webometrics ranking of universities also uses links as one of its indicators of universities' online presence (Aguillo, Granadino, Ortega, & Prieto, 2006).

Link relationship mapping is normally carried out for web sites rather than for web pages and results in some kind of diagram illustrating the relationships between the sites. The goal of the mapping may be exploratory: to get an overview of the web environment of the sites. Alternatively, the map may be used to formally or informally test a specific hypothesis, such as whether two groups of sites tend to interlink with each other or whether the interlinking within one collection of sites is denser than the interlinking within another collection of sites. Another purpose can be to identify the overall pattern of interlinking, such as whether there are one or more central sites or whether the linking reflects the geographic locations of the sites (Vaughan & Thelwall, 2005).

The following sections describe the techniques needed for simple link impact assessments and relational link analysis.

3.3   LINK IMPACT ASSESSMENTS

The basic premise for link impact assessments is that a count of links to a web page or a web site is a reasonable indicator of its utility, value, or impact. In parallel with citation analysis, the term *web impact* (sometimes shortened to just *impact*) is used to denote that which is represented by link counts. Starting with a collection of web sites, the data for a link impact assessment are the number of hyperlinks to each one from elsewhere on the web. The terminology *site inlink* (or external inlink) is used for the links sought: only those from outside of the web site being evaluated (i.e., excluding the internal site navigation links). These link counts have been easily available since the late 1990s from the search engine AltaVista via its advanced link search command *linkdomain*. This search command matches pages that link to any page within the web site having a specified domain name. For example, the search `linkdomain:news.bbc.co.uk` matches web pages that link to any page within the BBC News web site news.bbc.co.uk, and the search `linkdomain:webometrics.blogspot.com` matches web pages that link to any page within this blog. These searches are not perfect for webometrics, however, because they include linking pages both inside and outside of the target site. Fortunately, it is possible to modify the search to exclude the unwanted links from pages within the same site (called site self-links and unwanted for the reasons discussed above). These pages can be identified and subsequently eliminated using the *site* advanced search command.

The *site* command matches all pages with the specified domain. Hence, submitting the search command `site:www.microsoft.com` to AltaVista (it also works in Google, Yahoo!, and Live Search) returns a list of pages within the www.microsoft.com web site. The trick for link searches is to subtract these results from the linkdomain results. This can be achieved by placing a minus sign in front of the site command. All major search engines interpret the minus sign as an instruction to exclude results matching the subsequent keyword or search command. To obtain a list of pages that link to www.microsoft.com from outside the www.microsoft.com web site, the following single search should therefore be issued in AltaVista:

```
linkdomain:www.microsoft.com -site:www.microsoft.com
```

In other words, this is an instruction to AltaVista to identify all pages linking to any page in the www .microsoft.com web site and then to exclude from those results all pages within the www.microsoft .com web site and report the remainder. The following two searches use the same pattern.

```
linkdomain:news.bbc.co.uk -site:news.bbc.co.uk
```

```
linkdomain:webometrics.blogspot.com
         -site:webometrics.blogspot.com
```

In fact, the above searches are still not quite optimal. The reason is that large web sites typically have important subdomains, and these should be taken into account when constructing the searches. For instance, the www.microsoft.com web site may have derivative web sites with domain names like blog.microsoft.com, developer.microsoft.com, and search.microsoft.com. Hence, to be on the safe side, the search should be modified to encompass all these subdomains. Fortunately, this is possible because both the linkdomain and the site commands match the end of a domain name and so the search can be modified by truncating the domain name concerned to the part that sufficiently and uniquely identifies the whole web site (the truncation must be performed at a dot in the domain name though). In the above example, this would be microsoft.com, and so the final and best AltaVista search for pages that link to the Microsoft web site from other sites is the following:

```
linkdomain:microsoft.com -site:microsoft.com
```

Assuming that for the BBC News search the focus is only on BBC News and not on other aspects of the BBC, then it would not be desirable to change news.bbc.co.uk to bbc.co.uk for the linkdomain command, but it would be useful to make this change for the site command to remove any internal BBC links. Hence, the eventual AltaVista advanced search would be the following:

```
linkdomain:news.bbc.co.uk -site:bbc.co.uk
```

It would also be possible to modify the above search to exclude other BBC-owned sites like www .bbc.com by subtracting them, as follows:

```
linkdomain:news.bbc.co.uk -site:bbc.co.uk
                -site:bbc.com
```

The webometrics.blogspot.com search above does not need to be modified because it has no derivative subdomains. Although it is itself a derivative subdomain of blogspot.com, it would not make sense to exclude all links from blogspot.com because blogspot.com blogs are typically owned by different and unrelated individuals and so links between different blogspot.com blogs tend not to be in any sense internal site navigation links.

The linkdomain command discussed above currently works only in AltaVista and Yahoo!, both owned by the same organization. Yahoo! also maintains a Site Explorer interface that also gives information about links to a web site. Currently, Google, Yahoo!, and AltaVista also support the advanced search *link* command that matches all pages that link to a specified URL (rather than site); this is useful in webometric studies that are based on collections of web pages rather than on collections of web sites. The Google link search is not recommended, however, because it cannot be combined with the other commands like –site: and because it reports only a small fraction of the links known to Google.

3.3.1   Interpreting the Results

The following are guidelines for interpreting the data from an initial link impact assessment for a collection of websites. All the necessary raw data can be provided by LexiURL Searcher reports from site inlink searches for all of the sites or pages investigated.

- Compare the overall hit counts to discover which pages or sites have attracted the most links, notice any particularly weak or strong performers and comment on why they might be weak or strong.
- Identify the most popular types of site linking to each page or site (e.g., news, blogs, universities) and comment on why they might be popular.
- Identify *differences* in the most popular types of site between the different pages or sites and comment on why the differences might be there. Are any of the differences surprising or glaring omissions? For instance, an academic document not attracting links from any universities could be surprising.
- Identify the countries most often linking to each page or site (e.g., from the TLDs of the results, ignoring .com, .net, .org) and comment on why they might be hosting so many links.
- Identify differences in the most popular countries between the different pages or sites and comment on why the differences might be there. Are any of the differences surprising or glaring omissions? For example, perhaps one site has attracted much attention in the United States or another page is the only one not linked to from Mexico.

3.3.2 Alternative Link Counting Methods

Once searches have been designed to gather the link data, a decision should be made about whether to use the reported hit count estimates on the results pages, the list of matching URLs reported, or to calculate how many different sites are in the list of matching URLs. This parallels a similar decision for web impact reports. The simplest statistic to gather is the hit count estimates reported on the first results pages, but recall that this can be considerably different from the actual number of matching URLs returned. It is not true that the number of URLs returned is a more accurate statistic than the hit count estimates, because the former is likely to be a significant underestimate because search engines filter results to eliminate similar pages and too many pages from the same site (see Chapter 7 on search engines).

The best statistic is the number of linking web sites because of the possibility of repeated links within a site, for example, if a link acknowledging collaboration, web site design, or funding is placed on every page of an organization's web site. The number of linking sites can be calculated by manual checking of the number of different domain names represented in the URLs of the results. This process can be automated with appropriate software like LexiURL Searcher but, whether manual or automatic, the ability to count domains is dependent on there being fewer matching URLs than the maximum returned by a search engine, which is normally 1,000. If there are more results than this, then the query splitting technique discussed in succeeding parts of this book can be used.

Once the link count statistics have been obtained, they can conveniently be reported in a graph or table for ease of comparison, unless they are used in a specialist statistical test. It should be remembered and reported that the counts do not report the whole web, just the part of the web covered by the search engine used, and also that the search engine may not reveal all the information that it knows.

Webometric link analysis studies sometimes also use web crawlers or automatic search engine queries to gather data, and these are discussed in succeeding parts of this book.

3.3.3 Case Study: Links to ZigZagMag.com

This section presents a brief summary of a web impact evaluation of a web site. This evaluation was carried out to assess the web impact of the BBC World Service Trust's ZigZagMag youth culture magazine web site that was part of its Iranian journalism training project. An overall assessment of the impact of ZigZagMag was made in comparison to the most popular similar web sites in Iran, as identified by ZigZagMag users. Table 3.1 reports the results. The number of pages linking to each site was identified by LexiURL Searcher queries submitted to Yahoo! (e.g., `linkdomain: haftan.com -site:haftan.com` for the first search), using query splitting to gain additional matches beyond the first 1,000. The main impact statistic used was the number of web sites linking to each of the 12 sites, counted by domain name. The results showed that the web impact of

TABLE 3.1: A comparative impact evaluation of ZigZagMag through counts of links to its web site and to the best-known similar web sites

WEB SITE NAME AND GENRE	ESTIMATED NO. OF PAGES LINKING TO SITE	ESTIMATED NO. OF SITES (DOMAIN NAMES) LINKING TO SITE	ESTIMATED NO. OF TLDS LINKING TO SITE
Haftan—online portal	31,300	1,556	22
Balatarin—news sharing site	57,400	1,455	28
7Sang—online magazine	11,900	1,250	32
Meydaan—women's rights site	9,940	821	35
Sobhaneh—online portal	9,320	633	21
40cheragh—weekly magazine	18,700	594	14
ZigZagMag (ZigZagMag.com)	64,300	575	21
Radio Zamaneh	6,530	468	18
Rang—online magazine	9,330	346	14
Jadid Media (jadidmedia.com)	7,350	251	17
Jadid Media (jadidonline.com)	3,270	224	20
ZigZagMag (ZigZagMag.net)	48,400	91	14

ZigZagMag was comparable to that of the top similar web sites in Iran and that it was therefore a highly successful site, especially given its relative youth.

3.4   CONTENT ANALYSIS OF LINKS

As with web impact evaluations, a content analysis of a random sample of the links is highly desirable to be able to interpret the link counts. Without this, the significance of the link counts in Table 3.1 could only be described in very general terms. The classification should be conducted as discussed for web impact assessment but focusing on the context of each link in the page containing

TABLE 3.2: Results of a content analysis of 100 random links to U.K. university home pages (Thelwall, 2003).

TYPE OF PAGE/TYPE OF LINK	COUNT
General list of links to all university home pages	16
Regional university home page link list	2
Personal bookmarks	2
Subject-based link list	5
Other link lists	6
Personal home page of lecturer	
Link to degree-awarding institution	8
Link to previous employer	6
Link to collaborator's institution	3
Other	3
Collaborative research project page/link to partner site	17
Other research page	
Link to collaborator's institution	3
Link to institution of conference speaker	2
Link to institution hosting conference	2
Other	3
Link to home institution of document author	7
Collaborative student support	10
Other type of page	5

it. The content analysis should shed light on why the links were created using categories that are meaningful for the objective of the link impact study. See Section 2.3 (Content Analysis) for more details.

In some cases the content analysis rather than the link counts can be the objective of a link analysis. For example, one study attempted to find out why political web sites used hyperlinks. The findings included that these links were much more often made to like-minded sites than to opposing sites to engage in debate. Links also appeared to be included sometimes in apparent imitation of other web sites (Foot & Schneider, 2002). Table 3.2 summarizes the results of another content analysis study. The objective was to identify the types of reasons why links were created to university home pages in the belief that some of these links were fairly trivial. In support of this, the categories include some for links that it was argued were unlikely to be useful for the source page visitors, such as a link to a person's previous employer or their degree-awarding institution.

3.5   LINK RELATIONSHIP MAPPING

It is sometimes useful to illustrate the interlinking pattern within a collection of web sites. The natural form for this is a network diagram with small circles (or nodes) representing web sites and arrows between the circles representing the links between them. Starting with a collection of web sites, the data needed for a standard link relationship map are the number of links between each pair of web sites, counted separately for each direction of links. The data can be obtained from AltaVista using a combination of the advanced search commands *linkdomain* and *site*. The search pattern `linkdomain:A site:B` matches pages in web site B that link to web site A. For instance, the following search in AltaVista would return pages in news.bbc.co.uk that linked to the www .microsoft.com web site.

```
linkdomain:www.microsoft.com site:news.bbc.co.uk
```

This search is similar to the form used for link impact calculations except that there is no minus sign before the site: command and the two domain names are always different. To search for links from www.microsoft.com to news.bbc.co.uk, the order of the domains is reversed as follows:

```
linkdomain:news.bbc.co.uk site:www.microsoft.com
```

As in the case of link impact measures, it may be better to replace full domain names with the shortest part uniquely identifying the web site. In the above example, news.bbc.co.uk might not be changed if the focus is on BBC news, but the other domain could be shortened to microsoft.com.

For the link impact searches, the recommended counting method is to count pairs of interlinking sites rather than pages because of the problem of unwanted replicated links in some sites. This method could be applied to the data gathered as above, but because only two domains are involved in each search, the result would always be one link or zero link. In some cases the strength of connections between pairs of sites is important, however, and so link pages can be counted directly from the results or the hit count estimates on the results pages could be used instead.

If many web sites are involved in a study, then it could take a long time to calculate the number of links between them because of the number of searches needed. Mathematically, if there are n web sites, then $n^2 - n$ link searches are needed to get all the link counts. For example, 10 sites would need $10^2 - 10 = 90$ searches, but 100 sites would need too many to run by hand: $100^2 - 100 = 9{,}900$. Such searches can be automated for large numbers of sites, however, as discussed in Chapter 5 (Automatic Search Engine Searches: LexiURL Searcher).

The key issue for link relationship mapping is how to graph the results. The following list gives a range of common options, roughly in ascending order of complexity. The list is not exhaustive and more exotic techniques are always possible. If software like LexiURL Searcher is used to gather the data, then the same software can directly produce the visualization or save the data in a format suitable for importing into Pajek or another network drawing program.

- A *simple network diagram* with circles representing web sites (or pages) and identical arrows representing links between web sites. This kind of illustration could be drawn with any graphical software package, such as Corel Draw or Microsoft Paint, or with a specialist network analysis package, such as Pajek (Holmberg & Thelwall, 2009). To make large network diagrams as easy to interpret as possible, it is desirable to position web sites close together if they interlink and further apart if they do not interlink. In addition, the positioning should try to minimize crossovers between arrows. If a network analysis program like Pajek is used to produce the graph, then its network layout algorithms like Kamada–Kawai (1989) or Fruchterman–Reingold (1991) can be used as they partially achieve these goals.

- A *node-positioned diagram* is a network diagram in which the circles representing web sites (often known as nodes in network terminology) are positioned to convey information about interlinking through the positioning. This is particularly important for diagrams in which there are many nodes and so the "shorthand" of node positioning helps to reveal linking patterns. Statistical node-positioning techniques, such as the multidimensional scaling, can also be used to position the nodes (Vaughan & Wu, 2004). In this type of diagram, the links between sites are often not drawn because the position of the nodes conveys the necessary interlinking information.

- A *geographic network diagram* is a network diagram in which the circles representing web sites (i.e., the nodes) are positioned on a geographic map showing their origins to highlight geographic linking patterns (Ortega & Aguillo, 2009).

Network diagrams are most suitable for small or medium-sized networks. If there are too many web sites, then it can be impossible to see any pattern in the visualization because there are so many arrows that they all overlap and so the node-positioned diagram is more suitable. For any of the above types of network diagram, the appearance can be customized to provide additional information.

- *Variable arrow widths*: setting the width of the arrows to be proportional to the number of links between the source and target web site is useful if the number of links is an important factor. A threshold minimum number of links for a line to be drawn can be set so that the thinnest lines are omitted. There are alternative ways in which line widths can be calculated, which are especially useful for web sites of significantly varying sizes. For example, the widths could be divided by the number of pages in the source web site, the target web site, or both (Thelwall, 2001a). This avoids the results being dominated by the largest sites.
- *Variable nodes*: the appearance of nodes can illustrate properties of the associate web sites. For instance, the area of the circles representing the web sites could represent their sizes or inlink counts. Different shapes or colors can also illustrate properties such as the type of organization owning the web site or its country of origin (for several examples, see Heimeriks, Hörlesberger, & van den Besselaar, 2003; Ortega & Aguillo, 2008).

In addition to constructing diagrams, it is also possible to calculate related statistics from network data, many of which originate or have equivalents from the field of social network analysis (Björneborn, 2006). The simplest statistics are the number of links to each web site and the number of links from each web site. These data can be used to find the web site with the most inlinks and the site with the most outlinks, which may be the key sites in the network. The average number of inlinks and outlinks per site can also be calculated as a descriptive statistic, and this can also be used to compare different networks.

Within the field of complex networks, there are many algorithms to calculate statistics from network data (Börner, Sanyal, & Vespignani, 2007; Newman, 2003), and these tend to be most useful for those seeking to model the dynamic forces underlying the creation of a network rather than to understand the network itself. Within computer science, there are also many sophisticated network visualization techniques that advanced users may wish to try (Chen, 2004), as well as methods to automatically identify clusters of similar sites within a network (Flake, Lawrence, Giles, & Coetzee, 2002).

3.5.1 Case Studies

This section introduces a few different types of network diagram to illustrate the range of visualization techniques available. In each case, little information is given about the underlying study because the diagram itself is of primary interest.

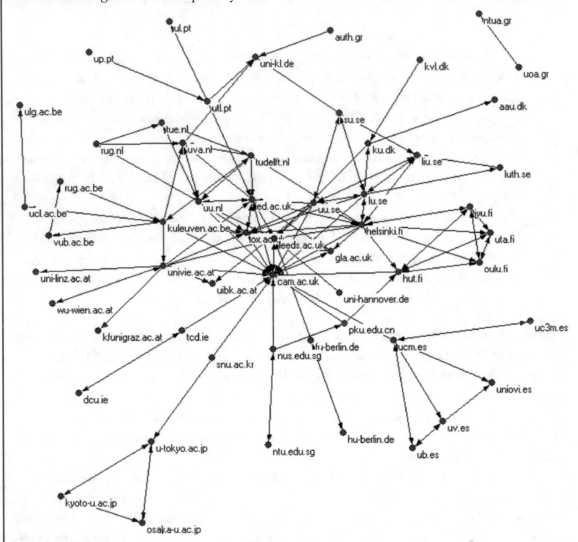

FIGURE 3.1: Simple network diagram of interlinking within the top European and Asian universities. Arrows represent at least 100 links, nodes are positioned using Kamada–Kawai, and unconnected universities are omitted (Park & Thelwall, 2006).

Figure 3.1 is a simple network diagram of interlinking between the top five universities in Asian and European nations with nodes positioned by the Kamada–Kawai algorithm. Without a positioning algorithm, the patterns in the diagram would have been difficult to detect because the lines would overlap too much. Most of the web sites interlinked and so a threshold of 100 links was used as the minimum to draw an arrow. Hence, this diagram shows the most frequently interlinking web sites. As an additional step for clarity, universities not connected to any others in the diagram were removed. The diagram is successful in the sense that patterns are relatively easy to distinguish. For example, it is not difficult to notice from the TLDs that universities from the same country tend to interlink and that U.K. universities form the core of the network.

Figure 3.2 is a variable arrow-width network diagram produced with Pajek. Each node represents all universities in a country, and the width of each arrow is proportional to the number of pages in the source country linking to universities in the target country. The use of variable widths for this diagram seems appropriate because there are not so many nodes that the widths would clutter the diagram. Nodes were positioned with Kamada–Kawai but manually repositioned afterward

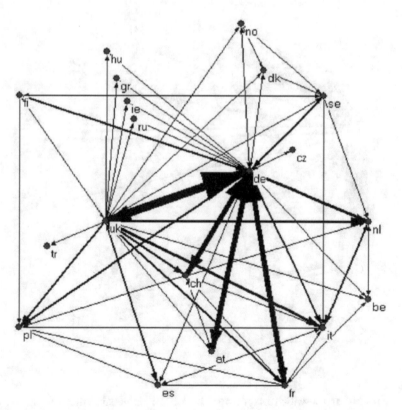

FIGURE 3.2: Variable arrow-width diagram of interlinking between European universities (Thelwall & Zuccala, 2008).

with small movements to reduce the number of line crossings and to ensure that node labels did not overlap.

Figures 3.3 and 3.4 are of similar data to Figure 3.2—European university interlinking—but are drawn in a different way. The universities are positioned in a circle at random and arrow widths are proportional to the number of pages in a given language (Swedish or Spanish) linking from universities in the source country to universities in the target country, divided both by the number of pages in the source and in the target country university system (because of the greatly differing sizes of web sites involved). A node positioning algorithm like Kamada–Kawai could have been used for these data, but it was judged not necessary because the pattern was clear from the circular graphs. The top diagram shows that Swedish interlinking mostly connects Sweden (se), Norway (no), and Denmark (dk), whereas the lower diagram shows that in European universities, Spanish interlinking almost exclusively originates within Spain.

Figure 3.5 is a multidimensional scaling map that does not include any arrows representing links but that uses link data to position the universities (the acronyms are web site names of

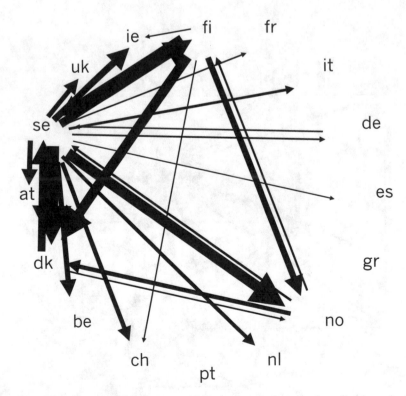

FIGURE 3.3: Variable arrow-width diagram of European university interlinking via Swedish pages (Thelwall, Tang, & Price, 2003).

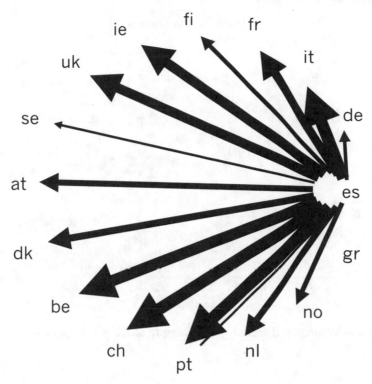

FIGURE 3.4: Variable arrow-width diagram of European university interlinking via Spanish pages (Thelwall et al., 2003).

U.K. universities). This approach, which clusters together universities that tend to interlink a lot, is appropriate because of the large number of web sites involved—too many to give details of each individual university.

3.6 COLINK RELATIONSHIP MAPPING

For some types of web sites, interlinking is rare and so they produce poor link networks. For instance, competing companies in the same market sector understandably seem almost never to link to each other. It may still be possible to generate a relationship map for such collections of sites using types of indirect links known as colinks (Björneborn & Ingwersen, 2004). Two web sites A and B are said to be colinked (or co-inlinked) if there is a page in a third site C that links to both A and B. On average, there are more colinks than direct links, and co-inlinks seem more likely to exist for similar companies than direct links. As a result, co-inlinks or co-inlink counts are useful for mapping sets of commercial web sites and also for other cases where there is not enough direct link data to generate a reasonable map (Vaughan & You, 2005). Most hyperlink-based mapping research has

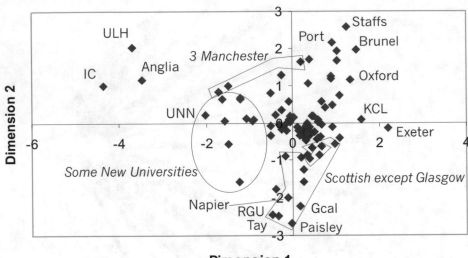

FIGURE 3.5: A multidimensional scaling positioning of U.K. universities according to the links between them (Thelwall, 2002b).

used colinks rather than links (e.g., Vaughan, 2006; Zuccala, 2006), although some have used both (Ortega, Aguillo, Cothey, & Scharnhorst, 2008).

The format of the colink search is linkdomain:A linkdomain:B –site:A –site:B, where A and B are the domain names of the web sites for which co-inlink counts are being obtained. In fact, this query matches pages that link to any page in site A and any page in site B but are not already in site A or site B. Fewer colink searches are needed than link searches [$(n^2 - n)/2$ for n sites] because this is a symmetric measure—although links can go either from A to B or from B to A, there is only one type of co-inlink between A and B. As a result, co-inlink network diagram should have lines rather than arrows between pairs of co-inlinked web sites. In most investigations using colinks, multidimensional scaling maps have been used instead of network diagrams, but there is no reason why a network diagram could not be used (Vaughan, 2006).

Figure 3.6 is an example of a co-inlink diagram, produced to illustrate the web environment of the ZigZagMag web site. For those who know the Iranian web(!), it shows that ZigZagMag associates strongly with Persian news sites and Persian blogs, and more weakly with international news sites and blogs and with other Persian sites.

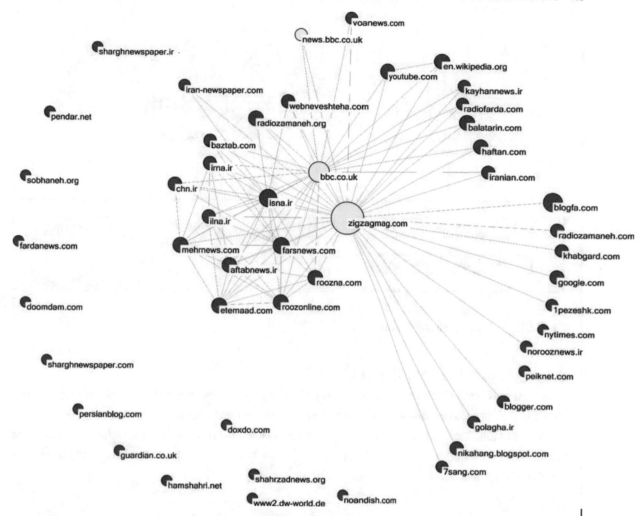

FIGURE 3.6: A co-inlink diagram of web sites linking to ZigZagMag.com, with lines connecting the most co-inlinked pairs of web sites, Fruchterman–Reingold positioning; circle areas representing total inlink counts; and light-shaded circles associated with the BBC (Godfrey, Thelwall, Enayat, & Power, 2008).

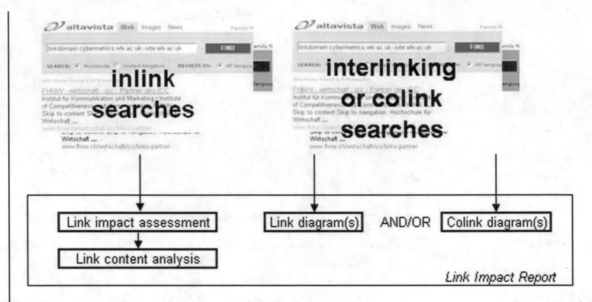

FIGURE 3.7: Link impact report data.

3.7 LINK IMPACT REPORTS

The data and analysis described above can either be used on its own or be combined into a report into the link context of one or more web sites, known as a web impact report (see Figure 3.7). The inclusion of a link or colink diagram is recommended even for reports that are exclusively concerned with link impact because network diagrams give a relativley easy to understand and attractive introduction to the web sites.

3.8 LARGE-SCALE LINK ANALYSIS WITH MULTIPLE SITE GROUPS

The principles described above can be applied to collections of groups of web sites if the link search commands are suitably modified. For example, to construct a network of interlinking between the Netherlands (nl), Belgium (be), and Luxembourg (lu), the following six searches could be used.

```
linkdomain:nl site:be
linkdomain:nl site:lu
linkdomain:be site:nl
linkdomain:be site:lu
linkdomain:lu site:nl
```

```
linkdomain:lu site:be
```

It is also possible to create a combined search for separate web sites by adding appropriate commands. To illustrate this, links from either main BBC site or Microsoft.com are captured by the following AltaVista advanced search, which uses the AltaVista Boolean keyword OR, which must be in capital letters.

```
(site:bbc.co.uk OR site:bbc.com) linkdomain:microsoft.com
```

All of the above diagrams that have nodes representing multiple web sites were produced using this type of advanced search.

3.9   LINK DIFFERENCES BETWEEN SECTORS— AN INFORMATION SCIENCE APPLICATION

This section briefly describes some link analysis research that is useful background for anyone designing a link analysis study. The underlying question is: are hyperlinks used in similar ways by everyone? A few studies have shown that there are significant differences between organizational sectors in the way that web links are created. This result can help manage expectations about what is possible from a link analysis. The differences are clearest in an investigation into hyperlinking between university, industry, and government web sites in the U.K. West Midlands. The results indicate that academic web sites contain far more links that the others, with commercial web sites containing the fewest.

It is part of academic culture to share information (e.g., in journal publications) and to draw on the work of others (e.g., in reference lists). This is true in both research and teaching. Hence, it seems natural for academic web sites to link to other web sites for information and to contain much information that other web sites could link to. In addition, academic hyperlinks are sometimes created to acknowledge a relationship, such as research collaboration or a government or commercial source of funding. Academic web sites also tend to be quite large and to have parts that are created and managed by various university members, such as staff personal home pages and research group web sites (Stuart & Thelwall, 2006; Stuart, Thelwall, & Harries, 2007).

Commercial web sites, in contrast, seem to be primarily marketing devices, designed to showcase a company's products or services and often controlled by the marketing department. In this context it does not make sense to link to competitors' web sites because this may cause loss of customers. There is hence an incentive to avoid having all links to other web sites. Nevertheless, some links may be created to a parent company, the web site design company, an online store for purchases, and useful supporting services (e.g., for related insurance).

In between these two extremes, government web sites (including local government) seem to be tightly managed but allow linking to acknowledge organizational structures, such as to parent or sibling organizations. In addition, there may be many public service links to useful and trusted sources of information (e.g., online health sites, bus timetables) or services (e.g., pest control, local attractions) (Holmberg & Thelwall, 2009).

In consequence of the above, link analyses based on hyperlinks between, to, or from academic web sites are likely to reveal clear patterns—perhaps related to information flows. The same is true for government web sites except that the patterns may reflect organizational structure and services instead (and hence show strong geographic trends) and the patterns may be weaker because of fewer links. In contrast, studies of links between commercial web sites are likely to be unfruitful. Links from commercial web sites may well also be unfruitful but could reveal organizational or symbiotic relationships between businesses. Links to businesses may be more interesting, but these could easily be dominated by links from online directories, which would undermine any patterns found. As describe above, one way to identify relationships between companies by link analysis is to use co-inlinks instead (Vaughan & You, 2005). This method estimates the similarity between two web sites by the number of web pages that simultaneously link to both (i.e., co-inlink counts). For a collection of business web sites, a similarity graph can be drawn, using the co-inlink counts between all possible pairs of sites.

3.10 SUMMARY

Link analysis is an approach for generating and analyzing data about the impact of information or organizations on the web, or the online relationships between documents, web sites, or organizations. The purpose can be either to directly study the web itself or to use the web as an indirect source of evidence about offline phenomena, such as interorganizational relationships. The data for link analysis can originate from commercial search engine searches or from research crawlers and can be reported in a variety of summary formats, such as inlink counts and network diagrams. Although link analysis seems relatively quick compared to most social science research methods, the results need careful interpretation with the aid of content analyses of links. Links can be an ideal source of up-to-date information and are particularly useful for pilot or large-scale studies and when used in conjunction with other methods (e.g., interviews) or data sources.

· · · ·

CHAPTER 4

Blog Searching

Blogs are web sites containing time-stamped postings written by one or more people and displayed in reverse chronological order. Blogs collectively form a fascinating new data source for social science research because there are so many of them—perhaps hundreds of millions—and they tend to be the informal thoughts or diaries of relatively ordinary people. For example, in principle, it would be possible to get a snapshot of public opinion related to any major topic by randomly sampling recent blog posts. Of course, bloggers are not typical citizens—they have Internet access and are probably relatively computer literate—but blog sampling can be achieved so quickly and easily that it can be a useful additional research technique for many investigations.

Blogs have a feature that makes them a unique data source for some social issues. The relative permanence of blog posts, due to old posts being archived online rather than deleted, make them a source of retrospective public opinion. It is possible to discover what bloggers thought about any topic at any point in the recent past simply by selecting posts from that period. There is no other large-scale accessible source of public opinion about major topics in the past other than about recognized issues via regularly administered standard surveys (e.g., national surveys of social attitudes). Without blogs, therefore, it would be impossible to answer questions such as: what did the public think about Barack Obama before he stood as a presidential candidate? when did the slang word *minger* become common in the United Kingdom? or when did the Danish cartoons affair become a major issue for the public of Western Europe? This chapter describes techniques for addressing such issues.

4.1 BLOG SEARCH ENGINES

The simplest blog investigation technique is blog-specific search engine keyword searching. By early 2009, there was a large choice of blog search engines, including Technorati, BlogPulse, IceRocket, and Google Blog Search (for a review, see Thelwall & Hasler, 2007). Each one can return results in reverse chronological order so that the most recent post is returned first. Figure 4.1 shows results for the search "Barack Obama" in Google Blog Search, with the first result being only 1 minute old. A less popular topic might find the first result being days or months old instead, however. A simple

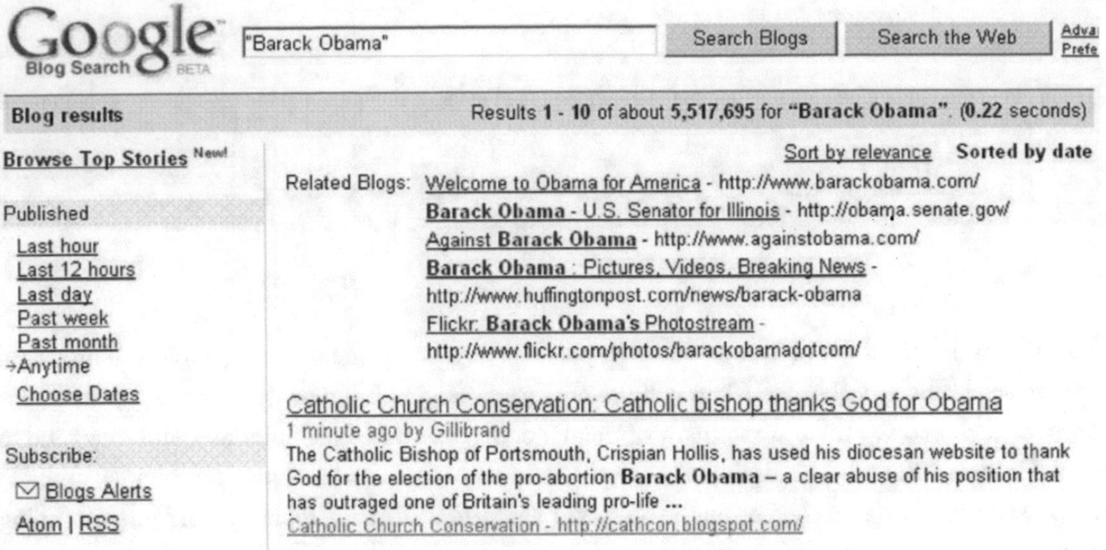

FIGURE 4.1: Google blog search results for "Barack Obama" in November 2008.

qualitative way to get an insight into public reactions to a topic, then, is to construct a suitable keyword search for the topic and spend some time reading through the matching blog posts. This could be formalized by conducting a content analysis of some or all of the matching posts (see elsewhere for more on content analysis).

The simple blog search has an important commercial application in market research, especially in support of marketing initiatives. A company that has just launched a major advertising campaign may want quick public feedback on its impact. One way it can do this is to search for relevant product or brand names in blogs and to read entries made after the start of the campaign. Computing organizations like IBM and Microsoft monitor large numbers of blogs so that they can automatically deliver relevant results to customers or allow customers to process the raw data themselves. In addition, specialist web intelligence companies like Nielsen offer a similar service. Organizations with a small market research budget could use blog search engines as a substitute.

4.2   DATE-SPECIFIC SEARCHES

The uniquely valuable information contained in the world's blogs is the time-stamped comments of a large number of ordinary bloggers. Several blog search engines, including those mentioned above, allow date-specific searches: normal searches but with a single day or range of dates selected for the results. Hence, it is possible to search for opinion about an issue 1 month or 1 year before it became major news. Of course, if nobody blogged about the issue before it became news, then there would be no blog search results.

As with standard blog searching, insights could be gained by spending time reading the blog posts in the data-specific search results or a more formal content analysis could be used. Unlike standard blog searching, however, there is normally no way of directly corroborating the results because there is no other large repository of public thoughts about any issue and humans are poor at recalling their past thoughts on an important topic. Hence, it may sometimes be that date-specific searches must be used unsupported as evidence for a hypothesis in research. In such cases, the researcher should discuss and evaluate the likelihood of bias in the blog data source. For example, they should assess whether an important constituency would be missing because it would have been unlikely to blog or would have blogged in a different language or in inaccessible blogs. The researcher should also mention in their report the weaknesses in blog searches as a data source, as discussed in this chapter.

In addition to date-specific searches, some blog search engines provide a range of advanced search facilities, typically on a separate page reached by clicking an "advanced search" link on the home page. These may include factors such as blog importance, language, and topic. Searches for blogs that link to a given blog are also possible in some search engines. All of these are probably less useful than the simple date-specific search for the typical researcher.

4.3   TREND DETECTION

A second unique feature of blogs, also derived from their time-stamped postings, is their ability to reveal trends in public opinion over time. This is supported in some blog search engines through the production of graphs of the daily volume of blog posts matching a keyword search. Currently, BlogPulse and Technorati offer this feature, covering the previous 6 months. To obtain such a trend graph, run a normal keyword search and then click on graph icon to request the production of an associated graph. Note that this is the first genuine webometric technique in this chapter in the sense of being quantitative.

Figure 4.2 illustrates the results of a search for `Cartoons AND (Denmark or Danish)` graphed by BlogPulse in May 2006 (Thelwall, 2007). The graph shows that interest in the Danish cartoons affair in English-language blogspace began around the 26th of January 2006. From then, it grew rapidly and then gradually subsided. The January start date is surprising because the cartoons were published on September 30 of the previous year. This generated media attention in Europe and condemnation by various Muslim groups and politicians but attracted almost no English-language blog posts before January (at least as reported by BlogPulse and corroborated by Google blog search). This seems to be strong evidence that the importance of the issue in the English-speaking world was not recognized at the time of publication and that other factors must

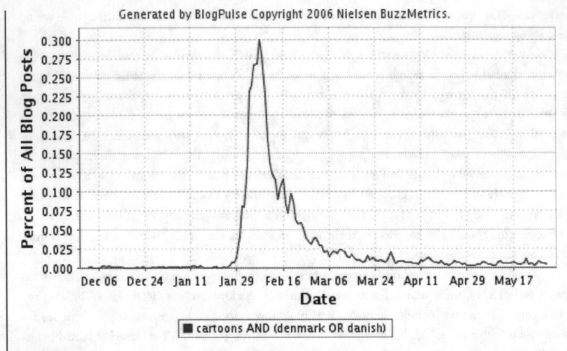

FIGURE 4.2: A blog trend graph of the cartoons debate: volume of blog postings related to the Danish cartoons debate (Thelwall, 2007).

have triggered the major debate. The evidence for this case appears particularly compelling because blogspace is a natural arena for airing and discussing important issues relating to politics and the news, and so it seems inconceivable that there would be a public perception of the importance of the Danish cartoons in the West without a corresponding significant number of English blog postings.

The BlogPulse Danish cartoons graph can also give evidence for the *cause* of the explosion in debate. Clicking on the start of the explosion on the 26th of January and just afterward gives a date-specific search for blog posts on the date. Reading these posts reveals two main events being discussed: the withdrawal of the Saudi Arabian ambassador from Denmark and the boycott of Danish food in Saudi Arabia. It seems that the coincidence of these political and economic events triggered the public debate.

Blog trend graphs, produced as above, are useful for several different related purposes.

- *Identifying the starting point for discussion* of an issue, verifying that an issue had not been significantly discussed before its assumed start date, or identifying bloggers who predicted or discussed an event before it became popular. The Danish cartoons graph illustrates this application, with blog posts at the trigger point revealing the cause of the explosion in discussion.

- *Identifying key events within a broad issue.* This can be achieved by constructing a keyword search for the broad issue (e.g., "stem cell research" or "abortion"), producing a blog search graph, and looking for spikes in the graph. Each spike is likely to represent a significant related news event that triggered blog discussions. For example, the Figure 4.3 spike on September 10, 2008, was triggered by discussion of stem cell research ethics as part of U.S. presidential election campaigning. These news events can be identified by running date-specific blog searches for the dates of the spikes (e.g., by clicking on the graphs). This technique works best for issues that occasionally generate significant blog discussions because the graphs produced by less popular issues are likely to be too spiky, dominated by random fluctuations in blogging rather than external events.

- *Identifying long-term trends.* A blog graph can reveal trends in the long-term interest in a topic—such as whether there has been an overall increase or decrease in interest over time.

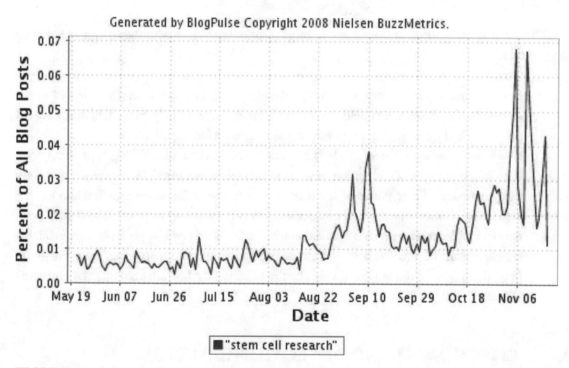

FIGURE 4.3: A blog trend graph of blog postings for stem cell research, indicating an apparent long-term increase in interest and at least two significant events.

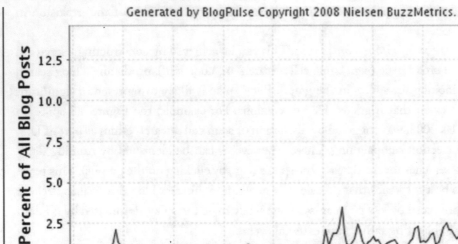

FIGURE 4.4: A comparison of the volume of blogs mentioning *Obama* with the volume mentioning *Obama* and *black*.

For instance, Figure 4.3 suggests that public interest in stem cell research increased in the second half of 2008. This could also be used, for example, to help gauge whether a retired politician had been quickly forgotten or had retained a lasting influence.

- *Comparative time series analysis.* It is possible to construct multiple blog time series with the explicit purpose of comparing how the trends relate. For example, Figure 4.4 compares the proportion of blog postings that mention *Obama* with the percentage that also use the word *black*. Comparing the two time series in the future, it may be possible to detect presidential incidents where race is invoked unusually frequently by bloggers. No such incidents are clear from Figure 4.4, however, although precise measurements taken from the graph (e.g., the height of the top line divided by the height of the bottom line) might reveal some unusual ratios.

4.4   CHECKING TREND DETECTION RESULTS

When using blog trend graphs, two further techniques are useful to check the results: keyword search testing and search trend comparison. Keyword searches should always be tested by reading a random sample of matching blog posts to ensure that most posts discuss the desired issue. Without testing, it is possible that the trends graphed may be unrelated to the desired issue. For example, if the Danish cartoons graph had been produced with the single keyword "cartoons," then it would have contained a second bump caused by an international cartoon convention.

Search trend comparison means using general search volume graphs, like those produced by Google Trends (www.google.com/trends), to produce parallel graphs to the blog trend graphs so that the shapes and key dates can be compared. This corroborates the blog information with general search information to assess whether the phenomenon is specific to blogs. The Google trends tool shows the daily volume of Google searches matching the keywords. In the Danish cartoons case, the shape of the blog graph Figure 2.2 is replicated by the Google Trends search volume graphs for the keyword search *Danish cartoons* (Figure 4.5). Of course, the two graph shapes will not always match as there may be topics that people search for but rarely blog about. Google Trends graphs are ostensibly a more authoritative source of evidence about trends in public opinion than blog graphs because more people search with Google than keep a blog. Nevertheless, Google Trends graphs cannot be validated by finding the cause of the searches graphed in the same way that blog trend graphs can be validated by reading the underlying blog posts from the graph. Hence, Google Trends graphs are best used to corroborate the blog trends graphs rather than as primary evidence.

Google Insights for Search is a similar but more powerful tool (www.google.com/insights/search) that can give some insights about why Google users have searched for particular terms by showing related terms.

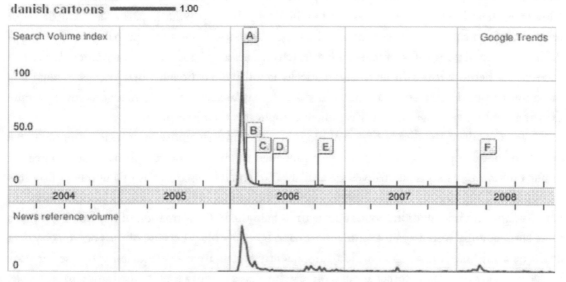

FIGURE 4.5: A Google trends graph of the volume of *Danish cartoons* searches.

4.5   LIMITATIONS OF BLOG DATA

A disadvantage of blogs as a data source for public opinion was introduced above: that bloggers are atypical citizens to some extent. This should not be exaggerated for developed nations because most have Internet access in one form or another and a small but significant proportion of the population have kept a blog (Lenhart, Arafeh, Smith, & Macgill, 2008). This proportion would be larger if the blogs of large social network sites like MySpace were included, although they are not (currently) open to blog search engines.

A second disadvantage of blogs in practice is that the coverage of blog search engines tends not to be reported and so there is an unknown bias in blog search engine results. Because blog search engines need to be engineered to process each different blog format efficiently, it is likely that only the most common formats are supported. Fortunately, this probably includes most or all large free blogging sites like blogger.com, but it may exclude all individually designed blogs. Moreover, blog search engines may include blogs with a Really Simple Syndication feed or similar because these are easy to process. In addition to these considerations, a blog can only be included if a blog search engine has found it. It may find blogs by a range of methods, including user submission of URLs and following links. These methods are likely to favor more popular blogs because their owners are more likely to promote them and others are more likely to link to them. Non-English blog formats are also less likely to be included because of the difficulty for U.S.-based blog search engine programmers in understanding them.

An important limitation of blog searching, for international issues, is that it is normally language-specific, with the exception of proper nouns and accepted international expressions. Moreover, there is variation in the extent to which blogging is popular in particular countries—for example, it seems particularly common in the United States and Iran but is probably rare in most of Africa because of poor Internet access. Blog search engines are almost always international in coverage—partly because it is difficult to automatically identify the nationality of a blogger because it is often not reported—and so the results of any search may include results from an unknown proportion of an unknown range of countries, which complicates their interpretation.

As a result of the disadvantages of blogs in terms of their ability to provide a representative sample of public opinion, they are not recommended as an unsupported primary data source for public opinion research if alternatives are available but could be used as one of a number of sources of evidence. They can also be particularly useful as part of an initial exploratory research phase, to gain background information about an issue or to help the initial formation of research hypotheses to be subsequently tested against more robust data. Ignoring blogs because of the poor-quality data could be a mistake if a research project subsequently suffers from inadequate hypotheses or poor background knowledge. Another use of blog searching is as part of a longitudinal study, for example, taking weekly samples of blogs, in which the task of identifying changes would cancel out some of the limitations of the data source.

4.6   ADVANCED BLOG ANALYSIS TECHNIQUES

All the blog analysis techniques discussed so far use freely available blog search engines and are easy to set up and use. For some purposes, however, more sophisticated tools operated by the researcher may be needed to produce the necessary results. This may involve a considerable increase in effort and difficulty. Blog search engines collect data daily on millions of blogs, and this requires considerable computing resources in terms of software development, computing power, and bandwidth. As a result, this undertaking seems justified for a researcher only if it would give the main evidence for a research investigation. This section gives some ideas about using blog monitoring and analysis programs.

- *Automatic spike detection in broad issue scanning.* The visual spike detection technique discussed above for identifying key events within a broad issue can be automated. If a large collection of blogs is monitored daily, then a blog search program can be written to match all posts relating to a broad issue, for example, via a general keyword search for the issue. It is then possible to detect overall spikes via testing for increases in the volume of matching blog posts. This is an automated version of manual spike identification. More significantly, it is possible to monitor each word mentioned within each blog posting to identify if and when each individual *word* spikes (Thelwall & Prabowo, 2007). This technique can detect hidden spikes for a sub-issue of a large broad issue. Part of the power of this technique is that through its exhaustive search of every word, it is able to detect previously unknown sub-issues within the known broad topic. An example of this technique is a project to automatically detect public fears about science from blog postings. This project monitored tens of thousands of blogs, filtering for the broad issue through a keyword search comprising a list of synonyms of "fear" together with a list of synonyms of "science" and "scientist." This extracted blog posts expressing concern and mentioning science. Automatic scanning of these filtered posts revealed a range of new issues, including concerns about CISCO routers in the Internet, stem cell research events, and the Terri Schiavo medical case in the United States. The strength of this method is its ability to detect previously unknown events hidden in a mass of data, but its disadvantage is that it is most effective for events associated with distinctive and unusual words.
- *Vocabulary analysis.* Some research requires exhaustive lists of words in blog postings, for example, in linguistic analyses of word variations either for linguistic research or as part

of a wider investigation into the spread of ideas. These vocabularies can be constructed by collecting blog postings, extracting lists of words from all postings, and constructing a list (vocabulary) of all words found. This is a particularly useful technique when the words or word variations sought are not known in advance but can only be found by scanning word lists (Thelwall & Price, 2006). The method has been used in a project to find and explore the evolution of words that are derivatives of *Franken*—as a framing device in debates over genetically modified food (e.g., Frankensoya, Frankenwheat). The results may also suggest when each new word first appeared in blogs, which could be corroborated through commercial blog search engines.

- *Long-term trend graphs*. At the time of writing, none of the commercial blog search engines would produce a blog search graph for longer than the previous year. Hence, projects needing long-term graphs could either purchase the data from the blog search engine companies or collect their own data. The latter option is a major undertaking because at least 100,000 blogs should be monitored to give reasonable quality graphs for anything but the biggest issue. If too few blogs in the collection discuss an issue, then the graph produced is likely to be dominated by random spikes.

4.7   SUMMARY

This chapter discusses a range of research techniques related to blog searching. The first and simplest techniques are not examples of webometrics because they do not involve any counting but the remainder are. The techniques make blogs a useful data source for public opinion and in some cases give information that is not available elsewhere. Moreover, most of the methods discussed are relatively easy to carry out via commercial blog search engines. Nevertheless, blogs provide weak evidence in many cases because bloggers are not representative of the population and the topics they blog about are not likely to be always representative of the issues that the population considers important. Blog searching is probably most widely useful as a "quick and dirty" way of gaining insights into a public opinion topic, to investigate topics that cannot be addressed in any other way (e.g., retrospective public opinion), or in conjunction with other corroborating evidence such as from Google trends.

· · · ·

CHAPTER 5

Automatic Search Engine Searches: LexiURL Searcher

The previous chapters have so far introduced the main webometric techniques and described how to carry them out without the use of specialist software, although the need for software is mentioned in a few places for tasks that are difficult to do without automation. This chapter introduces a specialist tool for webometrics, one to automatically submit searches to search engines and to process the results.

An automatic search engine query submitter (not standard terminology) is a program that is capable of automatically submitting queries to search engines and then downloading, saving, and processing the results. Although there are several programs that can do this for webometrics, including VOSON (voson.anu.edu.au) and Issue Crawler (www.issuecrawler.net) (Rogers, 2004), this program focuses on LexiURL Searcher, a free Windows program available at lexiurl.wlv.ac.uk. Both the automatic downloading and processing capabilities are important to make medium- or large-scale webometrics possible, unless a web crawler is used instead.

Although it is possible to write a program to automatically submit queries via a web browser and save and process the results from the browser, automatic search engine query submitters typically use the web services set up by the search engines, known as applications programming interfaces (APIs). APIs typically allow 5,000–10,000 searches to be submitted per day, per computer, and return the results in a very computer-friendly format (e.g., XML). The results are not the same as the equivalent results in the online search pages (McCowan & Nelson, 2007) but often seem to be reasonably similar. Automatic search engine query submitters typically start by the user entering either a list of preformulated queries or information such as web page URLs or web site domain names that would allow the program to formulate the queries itself. The next stage is that the program submits the queries to the chosen search engine and saves the results. Finally, when the results are all gathered, they are processed and displayed in some format, such as a table of results or a network diagram. Sometimes the three stages are automatic and sometimes user actions are required between them. This chapter introduces LexiURL Searcher and gives examples of how to use it for common problems.

5.1   INTRODUCTION TO LexiURL SEARCHER

LexiURL Searcher is a free program designed to gather data from search engines via their APIs for webometric purposes. At the start of 2009, it could access Yahoo and Live Search via their APIs but can only access Google for people with an existing Google API key (Google has stopped giving out new keys). In addition to downloading data from search engines and saving the results in simple text files, LexiURL is able to process the data to produce reports or diagrams and can also help with generating link searches for a set of web sites or URLs. The common uses of the program can be accessed via the wizard that appears when it starts, and advanced features are accessible via its classic interface for those who wish to do something nonstandard or more complicated. The free version of LexiURL Searcher does not include the query-splitting capability because this can generate a lot of work for search engines. The professional version containing query splitting is available to researchers from the author without charge.

As introduced above, the typical LexiURL Searcher analysis contains three stages. First, the researcher must generate a plain text file containing a list of the searches to be submitted to a search engine. If link searches are needed, then LexiURL Searcher has features to help convert a list of URLs into appropriate lists of link searches. Second, LexiURL Searcher will submit these queries to a chosen search engine and save the results in a few simple files. Finally, LexiURL Searcher can process the simple results files to give more detailed and formatted results. The second and third stages can be automated by the LexiURL Searcher Wizard for a few standard tasks.

LexiURL Searcher automatically attempts to get the maximum number of URLs for each query, up to 1,000. Because search engines return results in sets or "pages" of 10, 50, or 100 at a time, to get the full list of results, LexiURL Searcher has to submit multiple queries, one for each page of results, and then merge all the results when saving or processing them. This process takes time and uses multiple searches from the daily API maximum—typically 20 searches per query. Hence, if the full URL lists are not needed, then LexiURL Searcher should be instructed to get only the first results page and not to get any subsequent pages. This is achieved by unchecking the Get all Matching URLs option in the Search Options menu.

5.2   LexiURL SEARCHER WEB IMPACT REPORTS

The three-stage process used by LexiURL Searcher to calculate basic web impact reports—to summarize the extent to which a set of documents or ideas are mentioned on the web—is supported by the wizard as described below. Note that the result is not a full web impact report, as described in Section 2.5 (Web Impact Reports), but contains the URL analysis part and lists of URLs for a content analysis.

For a web impact report, first download the program from the web site lexiurl.wlv.ac.uk. Second, create a plain text file with one search term or phrase per line. The easiest way to create a plain text file is to use Windows Notepad (normally accessed via Start|All Programs|Accessories|Notepad). Each line should contain one search term or phrase, as would be entered into Google for a single search, and there should be no extra spaces nor blank lines in the file. If any search is several words, then it can be put into quotes (straight quotes rather than smart quotes) to ensure that the words occur consecutively in any matching documents. For example, the following book list could be used.

"Link analysis an information science approach"

"Mining the web discovering knowledge from hypertext data"

"Information politics on the web"

Once the file is created, start LexiURL searcher and select the *Web Impact Report* option from the first wizard screen and click OK (Figure 5.1).

The second wizard screen requests the plain text file with the searches: click OK and select the file in the dialog box that appears (Figure 5.2).

LexiURL Searcher will start gathering data and after several minutes or half an hour will display a report in the form of a set of interlinked web pages. The main table, accessed by clicking the *Overview of results* link, contains the number of URLs, domain names, web sites, second or top-level-domains (STLDs), and TLDs matching each search term or phrase. All data in the report are derived from Live Search (Figure 5.3).

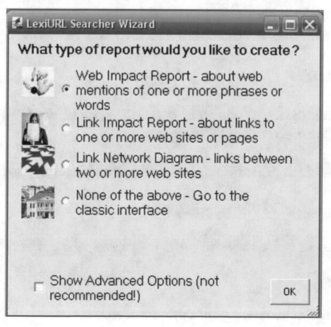

FIGURE 5.1: The initial LexiURL Searcher Wizard.

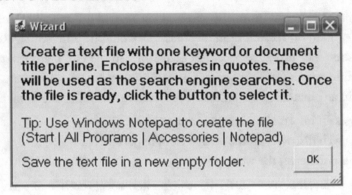

FIGURE 5.2: The second LexiURL Searcher Wizard.

A few less common types of web impact report can also be created but for this the classic interface will be needed rather than the wizards. The instructions below explain how to create a standard web impact report with the classic interface—this method can be customized for alternative reports.

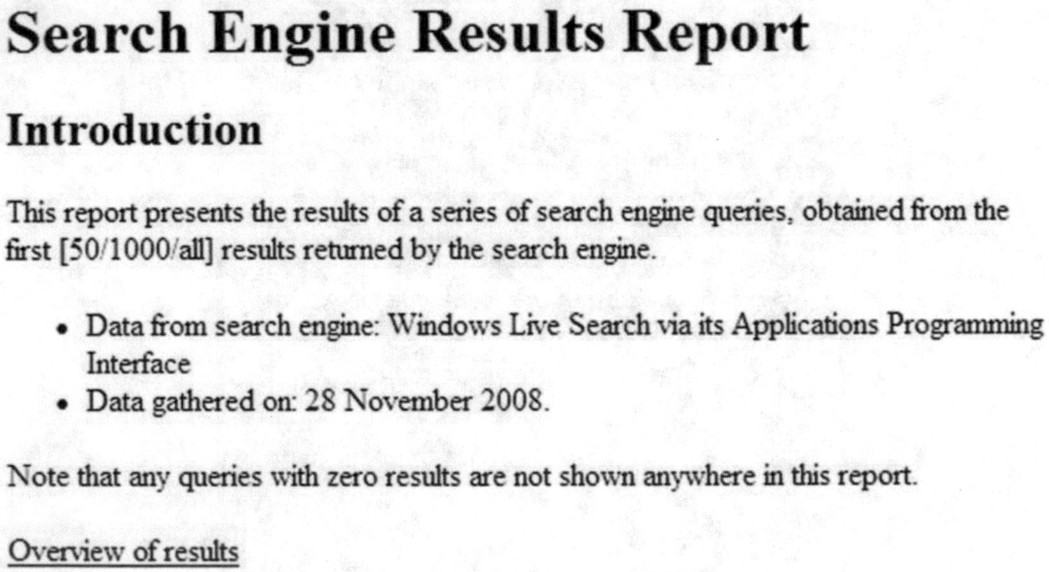

Search Engine Results Report

Introduction

This report presents the results of a series of search engine queries, obtained from the first [50/1000/all] results returned by the search engine.

- Data from search engine: Windows Live Search via its Applications Programming Interface
- Data gathered on: 28 November 2008.

Note that any queries with zero results are not shown anywhere in this report.

<u>Overview of results</u>

FIGURE 5.3: A section of the main page of a web impact report.

5.2.1   Web Impact Reports—Classic Interface Example

This section gives a step-by-step example of using the classic interface to create a web impact report. In brief, the user must construct a text file containing a list of searches, select a search engine and any search options, and then instruct LexiURL Searcher to start submitting searches and reporting the results. When the searches are complete, the user must select a processing option and instruct LexiURL Searcher to apply it to the appropriate results file. Below is a simple example to illustrate how this process works—it assumes that the program has been downloaded from lexiurl.wlv .ac.uk.

The example compares the web impact of three books: *Link Analysis: An Information Science Approach*, *Mining the Web: Discovering Knowledge from Hypertext Data*, and *Information Politics on the Web*.

- *Input data generation*. Create a text file containing the three book titles in quotes, one title per line. This file will be the input for LexiURL Searcher and the lines are each single searches. The quotes are included to ensure that the searches are exact phrase matches. The file should be constructed in Windows Notepad (Start/Programs/Accessories/Notepad) or a similar text editing program but not in a word processor. The resulting file might be called test.txt and contain the following contents.

  "Link analysis an information science approach"
  "Mining the web discovering knowledge from hypertext data"
  "Information politics on the web"

- *Running searches*. Start LexiURL Searcher classic interface and ensure that Live Search is the selected search engine by checking that this is the search engine ticked in the *Search Engine* menu. Move the file test.txt to a new empty folder in Windows to protect your computer from LexiURL Searcher accidentally overwriting or deleting files. Click the *Search* button and select the file test.txt. The searches will be submitted over a period of a few minutes, and LexiURL Searcher will report when they are complete. When the search is complete, three new text files will be found in the same folder as the original, with file names including "long results," "short results," and "result counts per page." If all that is needed is the hit count estimates, then these can be found in the short results file, shown below. The first number is the hit count estimates from the first results page and the last number is the actual number of URLs returned by the search engine. In this case the initial hit count estimates seem wildly inaccurate and the last column seems more likely to give reasonable estimates (see Chapter 7, Search Engines and Data Reliability, however).

450 "Link analysis an information science approach" 152

7840000 "Mining the web discovering knowledge from hypertext data" 729

90700000 "Information politics on the web" 310

If more information is needed than just the number of matching URLs, then this can be extracted from the "long results" file by using LexiURL Searcher features for producing reports based on search engine results.

- *Creating reports.* A standard set of summary reports can be produced from the raw search engine results in the "long results" file. This file lists the matching URLs returned, some text extracted from the matching page, and also repeats the search used. The number of URLs returned is never more than 1,000, which is the maximum returned by search engines. To create a set of standard summary reports, select *Make a Set of Standard Impact Reports from a Long Results File* from the *Reports* menu, select the long results file, and follow the instructions. This generates a set of web pages summarizing the searches, primarily an URL analysis. To view the results, double-click on the file index.htm in the new folder created to load it into a web browser. This web page lists the main summary statistics and gives links to the more detailed results. Figure 5.4 contains an extract from the overview. html page, which summarizes the main results.

As shown in Figure 5.4, the main table of a LexiURL Searcher impact report lists the number of URLs, domains, web sites, STLDs, and TLDs matching each search, as calculated from the long result files. This page can be reached from the main index.html page by clicking on the *Overview of results* link. The most reliable impact indicator is normally the number of domains rather than the number of URLs because of the possibility that text or links are copied across multiple pages within a web site. The results suggest that *Mining the Web: Discovering Knowledge From Hypertext Data* has

Overview of search results

Table listing the URLs of pages matching the queries submitted. In addition, it contains the number of domains, sites, STLDs and TLDs containing one or more URL matching the query, as derived from the URL list.

Name	Base query	URLs	Domains	Sites	STLDs	TLDs
-	"Link analysis an information science approach"	152	111	94	26	23
-	"Mining the web discovering knowledge from hypertext data"	729	560	452	80	54
-	"Information politics on the web"	310	234	191	36	33

FIGURE 5.4: Overview impact summary from a LexiURL Searcher report in the page overview.html.

the most web impact, based on its domain count of 560. The results also include full lists of matching URLs, domains, sites, STLDs, and TLDs for each query: clicking on the appropriate links on the home page reveals these lists. Figure 5.5 illustrates such a list: the top half of a table of domain names of URLs matching the second query.

Also included are random lists of URLs matching each search, with a maximum of one URL per domain. These are intended for use in content analysis classification exercises, as discussed in Chapter 2 (Web Impact Assessment). Finally, there is some information about the search at the top of the page, which can be modified in a web editor if necessary, and near the bottom of the home page is a link to a page with a comparative breakdown of TLDs and STLDs returned for each of the queries.

For ideas about how to interpret these data, see the bullet point list at the end of Section 2.1 (Web Impact Assessment Via Web Mentions).

It is important to note again that the results of an impact query do not give fair impact comparisons if the search engine has stopped giving results at 1,000. In fact, search engines sometimes

Domains of pages matching the base query: "Mining the web discovering knowledge from hypertext data"

The table lists the domains of pages matching the base query: "Mining the web discovering knowledge from hypertext data". The URLs column lists the number of URLs returned by the query with the given domain.

Domain	URLs	%
mse.sem.tsinghua.edu.cn	3	0.4%
www.zbh.uni-hamburg.de	3	0.4%
hpc.isti.cnr.it	2	0.3%
www.vbyte.com	2	0.3%
dblab.ssu.ac.kr	2	0.3%
www.5yiso.cn	2	0.3%
webspace.ulbsibiu.ro	2	0.3%
www.di.unipi.it	2	0.3%
www.ricercaitaliana.it	2	0.3%

FIGURE 5.5: Part of a table of domains matching a search from the LexiURL Searcher report page domains2.htm.

stop after about 850 unique results and so it is reasonable to be safe by only relying on the results if all the URL counts are below 850. See the chapter on query splitting techniques for searches with more results than this (Chapter 9).

5.3   LexiURL SEARCHER LINK IMPACT REPORTS

A link impact report can be created in a few steps with LexiURL Searcher, but note that the result is not a full web impact report, as described in Section 3.7 (Link Impact Reports), but contains the URL analysis part and lists of URLs for a content analysis. First, download the program from lexiurl.wlv. ac.uk. Second, create a plain text file with one domain name or URL per line, using Windows Notepad or similar. Each line should contain just the domain name of the web site and not any additional file or path information, and there should be no extra spaces in the file nor blank lines. The only exception is that if a web site shares its domain name with another web site, then the full URL of the home page of the site should be given rather than the shared domain name. Once the file is created, start Lexi-URL searcher and select the *Link Impact Report* option from the first wizard screen and click OK.

The second wizard screen requests the plain text file with the domain names and/or URLs: click OK and select the file in the dialog box that appears. LexiURL Searcher will then start gathering data and after several minutes or half an hour will display a report in the form of a set of interlinked web pages. The main table, accessed by clicking the *Overview of results* link, contains the number of URLs, domain names, web sites, STLDs, and TLDs linking to each web site. For the rows in the table containing web sites with just a domain name, the figures are for links to anywhere in the web site, but for web sites with additional path information, the figures are for links to just the specified URL. All data in the report are derived from Yahoo searches.

A few less common types of link impact report can also be created, but for this the classic interface will be needed rather than the wizards. The instructions below explain how to create a standard link impact report with the classic interface—this method can be customized for alternative reports.

For information about how to conduct a simple analysis of this data, see the bullet point list at the end of the introductory part of Section 3.3 (Link Impact Assessments).

5.3.1   Link Impact Reports—Classic Interface Example

The instructions in Section 5.2.1 for web impact reports apply almost without change to link impact reports. To create a link impact report, a list of URLs or domain names can be fed into LexiURL Searcher and it will download a list of pages that link to them, via search engine searches, and then produce a summary report based on the URLs of these pages. The main difference is that the searches used are not phrase searches like "Link analysis an information science approach" but are link searches like

```
linkdomain:linkanalysis.wlv.ac.uk -site:wlv.ac.uk
```

as described in Chapter 3 (Link Analysis). In addition, the searches can only be carried out with Yahoo! because the other search engines do not allow them.

5.4   LexiURL SEARCHER FOR NETWORK DIAGRAMS

LexiURL Searcher can support all of the stages of gathering and processing data to produce a network diagram for the links between a collection of web sites. This process is supported by the LexiURL Searcher Wizard. First, download the program from the web site lexiurl.wlv.ac.uk. Second, create a plain text file with one domain name per line using Windows Notepad or similar. Each line should contain just the domain name of the web site and not any additional file or path information, and there should be no extra spaces nor blank lines. For example, the file might contain the following two lines.

```
cybermetrics.wlv.ac.uk
lexiurl.wlv.ac.uk
```

Once the file is created, start LexiURL searcher and select the *Network Diagram* option from the first wizard screen and click OK. The second wizard screen requests the plain text file with the domain names: click OK and select the file in the dialog box that appears. Once the file is selected, LexiURL Searcher will start gathering data and when this is finished will display a network diagram in a *SocSciBot Network* window, but this may take several minutes. The circles in the network diagram will have areas proportional to the number of pages in the web site that they represent, and the arrows in the network diagram will have widths proportional to the number of links that they represent. All data used to generate the diagram are derived from Yahoo searches (Figure 5.6).

Different network diagram variations can be created than the standard one. To create a co-inlink diagram instead of a direct link diagram (e.g., if the sites do not interlink), follow the same instructions as above, but in the first step, check the *Show Advanced Options* box and then an additional wizard dialog box will eventually appear. This will give the option to run co-inlink searches instead of direct link searches. Check this option and wait for the co-inlink diagram to be created.

5.4.1   Rearranging, Saving, and Printing Network Diagrams

The network diagrams produced in LexiURL Searcher (and SociSciBot, which uses the same graphing tool) can be rearranged, reformatted, saved, and printed. This section briefly describes the most common of these actions.

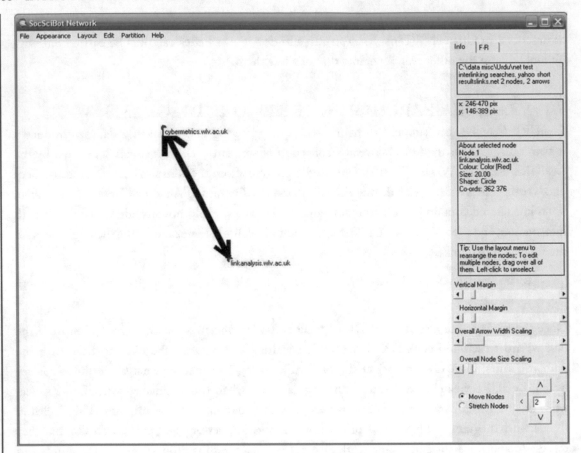

FIGURE 5.6: A simple network diagram created by LexiURL Searcher.

Once the network is displayed, it is important to arrange it so that it is readable and the patterns are easily visible to a human reader. To achieve this, the circles should be moved so that they do not overlap or intersect with lines and so that the lines themselves intersect as little as possible. It is also helpful to position circles close together if they interlink and further apart, as far as possible, if they do not. This rearrangement can be achieved manually or with the help of the Fruchterman–Reingold positioning algorithm. There are also many options to alter the appearance of the diagram in the main menus and right-click menus. For example, the right-click menus contain options for changing the color or the border color of the circles in the diagram. Most of the right-click formatting options are applicable by selecting one or more web sites (by dragging the mouse across them) and then using the right click button to access a menu of options.

The network diagram and positions can be saved by selecting *Save As* from the *File* menu and saving as a SocSciBot Network file type. Alternatively, the network can be saved as a Pajek network, although in this format less information may be saved.

A network can be printed using the *Print* option in the *File* menu. There are various ways in which a network can be included another document, such as a Word file. The options below list various ways, in increasing order of image quality.

1. *Paint bitmap*. Press the *Print Scr* button on the keyboard, load Microsoft Paint (Start|All Programs|Accessories|Paint) or similar, and press Control-V. This should copy the screen into the Paint program, where it can be edited down to the correct size. Once edited, the file can be saved (as a bitmap .bmp for the highest resolution or as a GIF .gif for the smallest file size) and then incorporated into a document (e.g., MS Word, using Insert|Image|From File).

2. *Medium-resolution TIFF*. Within the network program, select File|Print and then choose the Microsoft Office Document Image Writer printer driver from the Printer dialog box (in the Printer Name section). This prints a TIFF network diagram that can be inserted into a document, as for option 1.

3. *High-resolution TIFF*. A high-resolution TIFF printer driver is normally needed to get a higher-resolution file than 300 dpi. Once this is installed (it will probably have to be bought), follow the instructions for option 2 above, except selecting the new printer driver.

5.4.2   Network Diagram—Classic Interface Example

The classic interface rather than the wizard is used if less common types of link and colink diagram are needed. The instructions below explain how to create a standard network diagram with the classic interface with a small example, and this method can be customized for alternative network diagrams.

- Create a plain text file using Windows Notepad or a similar text editor containing a list of the domain names of each web site, one per line. For example, the file might be called smalllist.txt and contain the following list of domains.

```
www.yahoo.com
www.harvard.edu
www.wlv.ac.uk
```

- Use LexiURL Searcher's ability to generate a list of searches between all pairs of sites by selecting *Make Set of Link Searches Between Pairs of Domains* from the *Make Searches* menu and selecting the list of domains just created (e.g., smalllist.txt). This creates a new text file (e.g., called smalllist.searches.txt) containing the necessary searches. The searches can be seen by opening the file.

- Select the Yahoo search engine by choosing Yahoo from the Search Engine menu—it is the only search engine that can run the link queries. In addition, from the *Search Options* menu uncheck the *Get all Matching URLs* option. For simple network diagrams, the link counts from searches will be used but not the full set of URLs returned from the search, and so the searching process is sped up by stopping the full set of results from being gathered by unchecking this option.

- Click the *Run All Searches in a File* button and select the file with searches in (e.g., called smalllist.searches.txt) and wait for the searches to finish. This may take several minutes, but for a large network it could take several hours.

- Once the searches are finished, the hit count estimates in the short results file can be used as the raw data for a network diagram. To convert the short results into a format that can be read by the Pajek or SocSciBot Network programs, select *Convert link or colink short results file to Pajek Matrix* from the *Utilities* menu and select the short results file (e.g., smalllist. searches. yahoo short results.txt). The new file created will be in the necessary format (e.g., smalllist.searches. yahoo short results.net). This can be loaded into Pajek, if installed on the computer, or can be viewed in SocSciBot Network.

- To display the network diagram, select SocSciBot Network from the *File* menu and the visualization screen will appear. From the new SocSciBot Network screen, select *Open* from the *File* menu and select the network file (e.g., smalllist.searches.shortresults.matrix.net). The network will then be displayed on screen in a random format.

5.4.3 Colink Network Diagrams

As described in Section 3.6 (Colink Relationship Mapping), colink diagrams are often more revealing than link diagrams because they present an external perspective on a collection of web sites and can reveal structure even if the web sites in question do not often interlink. If a colink network diagram is needed instead of a link network diagram, then the LexiURL Searcher Wizard can be followed as above for link networks but with the modification of checking the *Show advanced options* box and selecting co-inlink networks instead of link networks. If following the nonwizard steps, then a modification to step 2 is needed to create a file of colink searches. In webometrics terminology the searches needed are actually for co-inlinks and so the option *Make Set of Co-inlink and Co-*

outlink Searches from a list of URLs or Domains from the *Make Searches* menu should be used instead. This creates two files. In step 3, select the new file of co-inlink searches (ignoring the other new file) for the searches. Note that the lines drawn in a network diagram for colinks should not have arrows on because colinks do not have a direction.

5.5   LexiURL SEARCHER ADDITIONAL FEATURES

LexiURL Searcher contains numerous utilities and options that can be used for nonstandard or enhanced analyses. These typically involve a combination of menu item functions. Some of the key functions are described below but more will be added over time.

Combining results from multiple search engines. Sometimes it is important to get lists of URLs matching a search that are as exhaustive as possible. This can be achieved in LexiURL Searcher by running the same searches in Yahoo and Live Search (excluding link searches, which do not run in Live Search) and then combining the results. Although it does not make sense to combine the short results files, the URL lists in the long results files can be merged by using the *Merge two long results files with overlapping or identical queries* option in the *Utilities* menu and then selecting each of the files to be included. The resulting merged file has duplicate URLs eliminated and can be used as input for any LexiURL Searcher facility that processes the long results files. For example, when preparing a web impact report, the results of different search engines could be combined before selecting the *Make a set of Standard Impact Reports* option from the *Reports* menu to generate a more comprehensive report.

Creating network diagrams interactively. Network diagrams can be built site by site or page by page in SocSciBot Network, using its inbuilt menu and right-click menu options to download pages and add to the diagram the pages that they link to. For example, start SocSciBot Network from LexiURL Searcher's *Show SocSciBot Network* menu option in the *File* menu and start by deleting the default diagram by selecting *Delete the Whole Network* from the *Edit* menu. Now add a first page by selecting *Add New Node* from the *Edit* menu and entering the domain name cybermetrics. wlv.ac.uk as the node name. To add web pages linked to this one, select the new circle by dragging the mouse over it and select *Crawl (recursively download) from selected node(s) and add all links to diagram* from the right-click menu. Enter the crawl depth 1 (just follow links from the page), leave the search text blank, and wait for it to crawl and update the diagram.

Processing longer lists of searches. If more searches than the maximum daily total need to be processed, then LexiURL Searcher will stop just before the limit and produce a dialog box asking what to do. The easiest option is to wait 24 hours before clicking on the option and then increasing the search limit in the new dialog box by 4,500 (Yahoo) or 9,500 (Live Search), allowing the searches to continue. The 24-hour delay is necessary to obtain a new API limit "allowance" from the search engine, and it is a good idea to set the limit at a few hundred less than the daily maximum to be on the safe side of the limit.

Gaining more than 1,000 results per search. If there are more than 1,000 results for a search, then this is a problem due to the search engine 1,000 result URLs maximum. In the professional version of LexiURL Searcher, it is possible to gain extra matches using the "query splitting" technique. This option is not available in the free version because it generates many additional searches and so creates extra demands on the search engine used. Please email the author if you are a researcher and need this extra capability.

• • • •

CHAPTER 6

Web Crawling: SocSciBot

This chapter introduces the web crawler software that can download and process a set of web sites to extract key summary statistics or to visualize any interlinking between the sites. Web crawlers are an alternative to automatic search engine searches that are appropriate when conducting an in-depth analysis of a set of web sites or when more reliable data are needed than provided by search engines. Web crawler data are more reliable than that from search engines in the sense that the scope of the crawls is determined by the researcher, whereas the extent of coverage of any particular web site by a commercial search engine is unknown. Moreover, the data from webometric crawlers like SocSciBot 4 (available free at socscibot.wlv.ac.uk) are designed to be as accurate as possible for webometric purposes, whereas search engine results are optimized for fast and effective information retrieval rather than for accuracy.

6.1   WEB CRAWLERS

A web crawler is a program that can be fed with a single URL and then can download the web page, identify the hyperlinks within that web page, and add them to its list of URLs to visit. The web crawler can then repeat the above process for each new URL in this list and keep going until it runs out of new URLs or reaches some other predefined limit (e.g., crawling a maximum of 15,000 URLs). Small-scale personal web crawlers typically visit one site at a time, starting at the home page URL and identifying and downloading web pages within the same site. Once finished, the crawler will usually have identified and downloaded all pages within a web site that can be found by following links from the home page. It is important to note that crawlers can only find new pages by following links and so will miss pages that are not linked to. In a small, well-designed web site, a crawler should be able to find all pages, however.

Figure 6.1 illustrates the "findability" issue for web crawlers. In this diagram, circles represent pages in a web site and arrows represent hyperlinks between them. A web crawler starting at the home page A will be able to follow its links to find pages B and E. It will then be able to follow the link on page B to find page C but will never find pages D and F because none of the pages found link to them.

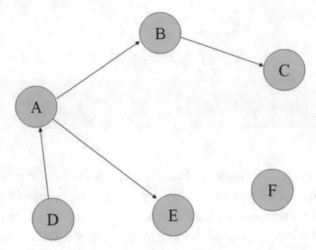

FIGURE 6.1: A simple web site link structure with circles representing pages and arrows representing hyperlinks. Pages D and F are not findable by crawling from A.

Web crawling can be used for relational link mapping. Suppose that a network diagram or other analysis of the links between a set of web sites is needed. The necessary data could be gathered by any web crawler if it was fed with the home page of each of the sites and tasked with crawling the sites as fully as possible. A webometric web crawler like SocSciBot (described below) can perform the downloading and also extract data about the links between the web sites crawled.

In Section 3.5 on link relationship mapping, the use of advanced searches in the search engine AltaVista was described as a method for finding links. A web crawler would, in theory, return the same results, but in practice, a web crawler would be more reliable for two reasons. First, the researcher can ensure that the web crawler visits all sites in the study, whereas a search engine may not have visited them all because search engines only cover a fraction of the web. Second, search engines tend not to report all results that they know about, hiding duplicate and near-duplicate pages (see Chapter 7, Search Engines and Data Reliability). In contrast, the figures returned by a web crawler will be an accurate reflection of the number of links that it has found. There are some advantages in using search engines instead of web crawlers, however, particularly for collections of very large web sites. Commercial search engines may cover more pages in large web sites than individual web crawlers because large web sites may become fragmented over time and hence no longer fully crawlable by a web crawler. A search engine may be able to find the fragments by knowing the URLs of pages from previous visits to the site when it was better connected (Thelwall, 2001b) or by following links from other sites. A second advantage is that crawling large web sites can take a long time and some web sites are too large to be practical to crawl with webometric web crawlers (e.g., www.microsoft.com or any large U.S. university web site).

6.2 OVERVIEW OF SocSciBot

SocSciBot is a web crawler designed for webometrics research. It has been used to collect and analyze data on sets of web sites for more than 50 research articles. It has three main features: a crawler, a link analyzer, and a text analyzer. In version 3, these three features worked as separate programs, but they are combined in version 4. SocSciBot must be used in two separate phases for any research project: crawling and analysis. The two phases should not run concurrently because data from the crawling can interfere with the results of the analysis. The following illustrates the three stages for any SocSciBot investigation.

- *Create a new project and give it a name.* SocSciBot can crawl multiple web sites and analyze them together, but the web sites must be collected into the same "project" for this to be possible. Hence, the first step with using SocSciBot, once it has been downloaded, is to create and name an empty project to contain all of the crawls. New projects can be created by entering a name in the SocSciBot Wizard Step 1 that appears when SocSciBot starts.
- *Crawl all the web sites to be analyzed together.* Once the project has been created, it can be populated by crawling the web sites to be analyzed within the project. New crawls can be added to a project by first selecting the project by name in SocSciBot Wizard Step 1 and then following the instructions in Wizard Step 2 to register the web site to be crawled.
- *Analyze the crawled web sites.* Once the crawls of all the web sites are complete, the downloaded data can be analyzed through the link analyzer, the text analyzer, or both. The links from web sites in a project can be analyzed by first selecting the project by name in SocSciBot Wizard Step 1 and then choosing the link analysis option in Wizard Step 2 to access a standard set of reports on the links.

6.3 NETWORK DIAGRAMS OF SETS OF WEB SITES WITH SocSciBot

This section describes how to use SocSciBot to crawl a set of web sites and then to construct a network diagram of the links between them. It uses SocSciBot 4.1, which is available free online from socscibot.wlv.ac.uk. The screenshots shown below are likely to change slightly in later versions of the program.

Step 1. Initiate a crawl of the web sites that are to be analyzed. This can be done in two ways. The easiest way is to run a simultaneous crawl of all sites. To achieve this, start by creating a plain text file containing a list of URLs of the home pages of the sites to be crawled, one per line. For instance, the file might be created with Windows Notepad (normally accessed via Start/Programs/Accessories/Notepad), called startlist.txt, and contain the following text.

```
http://linkanalysis.wlv.ac.uk
http://cybermetrics.wlv.ac.uk
http://socscibot.wlv.ac.uk
```

Note that the file should not be created with a word processor because such programs add unwanted codes to the files they create.

Step 2. Start SocSciBot and initiate the web crawls. Before starting SocSciBot, it is a good idea to download and install the free network analysis program Pajek, as SocSciBot looks for this only the first time it starts. Once SocSciBot starts for the first time, it asks for a location in which to save the data. Make sure that this is a place where you have permission to write or save data. This should preferably be in a hard disk on your own computer rather than a network drive as the latter can cause problems. SocSciBot then asks for a new project name (or to select an existing project, but the latter option can be ignored for now). Enter a project name such as "First test project" and press the *Start new project* button, as shown in Figure 6.2.

Step 3. Select a multiple site crawl or enter the URL of a single web site home page to crawl that site. Select the *Download multiple sites* option, as shown in Figure 6.3 (the other option is discussed below), and click the *Crawl Site with SocSciBot* button.

Step 4. Load the list of home pages of sites to be crawled. To achieve this, first select the option: "I have a list of home pages of web sites that are not too big and I want all the web sites crawled

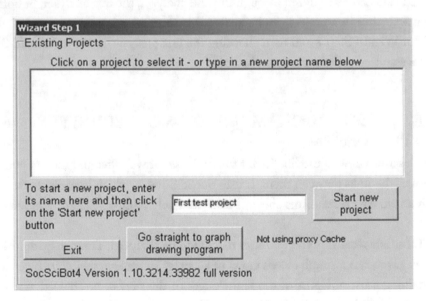

FIGURE 6.2: SocSciBot Wizard Step 1 showing a new project called "First test project" about to be created.

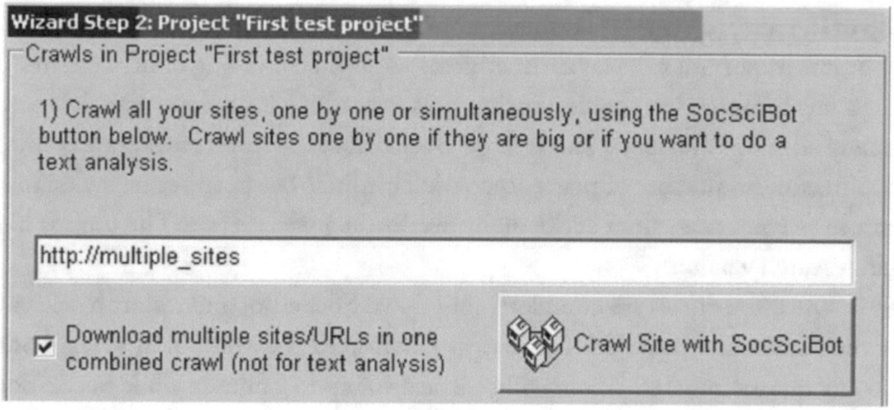

FIGURE 6.3: Registering to crawl multiple sites in a combined crawl.

completely in one go" option and then click on the *List of URLs to crawl* button and select the file startlist.txt created in step 2. The home pages and web site domain names should now appear in a list box at the bottom of the screen (see Figure 6.4). The domain names need to be checked because these indicate the scope of each crawl—that is, SocSciBot will crawl any URL matching these domain names but will ignore all others.

   Step 5. Start the crawl by clicking on the *Crawl Above List of Sites/URLs* button. If about a file locations, select the default folder. Before starting the crawl, read the contents of the ethics tab

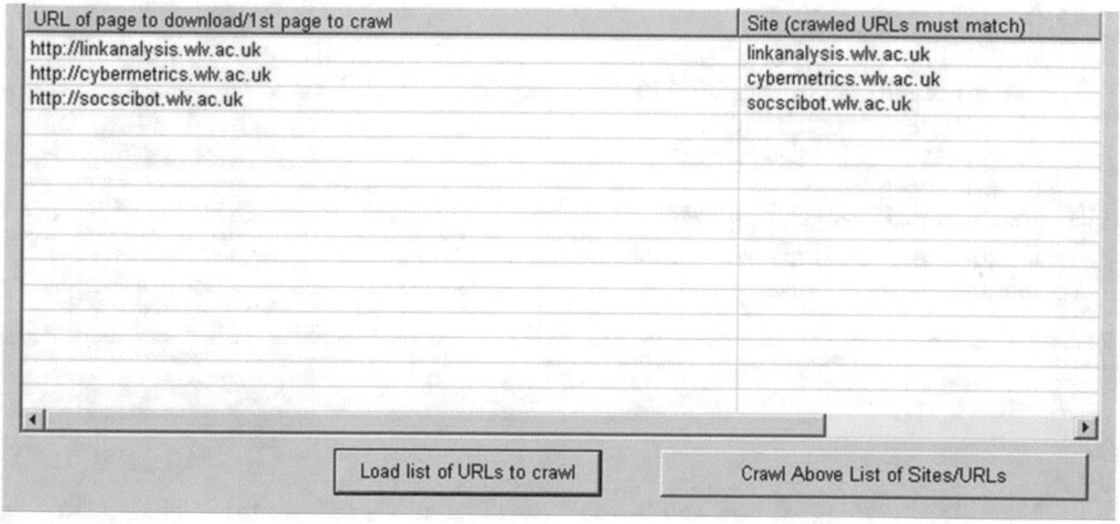

FIGURE 6.4: A list of home page URLs loaded for a multiple crawl.

near the top of the screen. There is no ethical problem with crawling the three sites above for testing purposes, but it is important to be aware of ethical issues when crawling other web sites. The crawls should take a few minutes, but crawls of other sites may take a long time—possibly several days if there are many sites or at least one site is large. SocSciBot may stop crawling early if it reaches its limit for the maximum number of pages to crawl. This limit has been set in the online version of the program to prevent users from accidentally overloading web servers. The limit is higher in the professional research version.

Step 6. Once the crawls are complete, shut down SocSciBot and restart it, select the project created for the crawls, and then click the *Analyse LINKS in Project* button in Wizard Step 2, replying "Yes" to any questions asked. There will be a delay of up to a minute while SocSciBot calculates a range of basic link statistics and then it will display a new screen from which the statistics can be accessed (see Figure 6.5). Clicking on a report name reveals more information about the report and gives options to load the report. Most of these reports are not needed for most analyses.

Step 7. Producing a network diagram. For this analysis, the focus is on producing a network diagram. Select the *Network Diagram for Whole Project* tab and click on the *Re/Calculate Network*

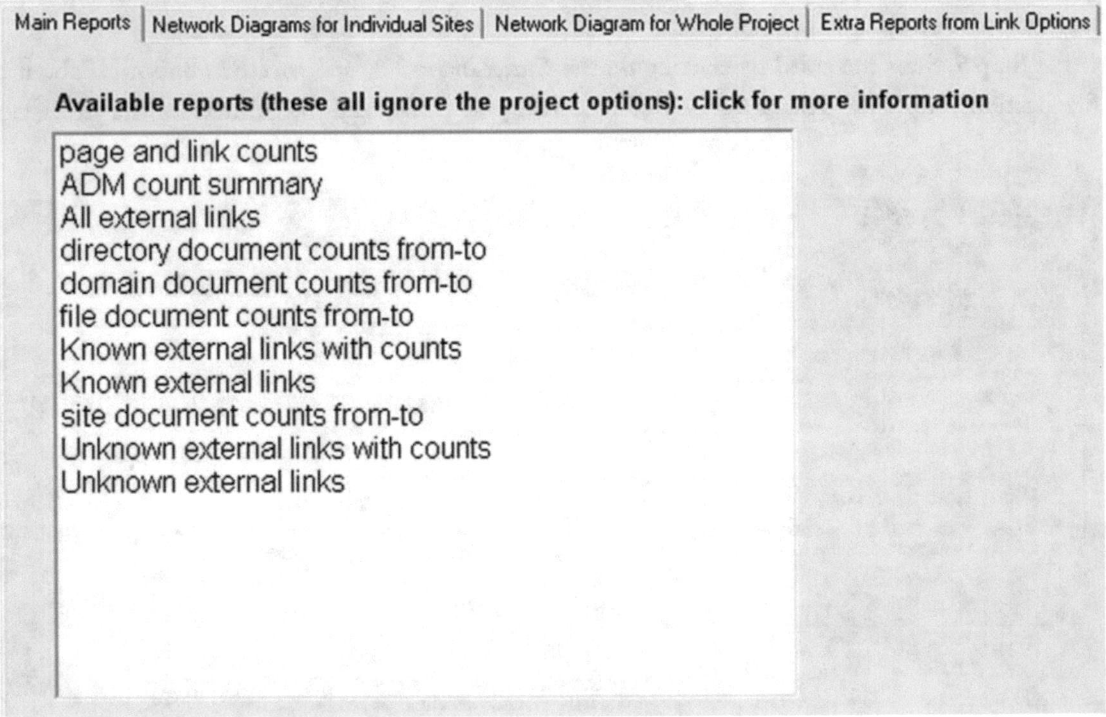

| Main Reports | Network Diagrams for Individual Sites | Network Diagram for Whole Project | Extra Reports from Link Options |

Available reports (these all ignore the project options): click for more information

page and link counts
ADM count summary
All external links
directory document counts from-to
domain document counts from-to
file document counts from-to
Known external links with counts
Known external links
site document counts from-to
Unknown external links with counts
Unknown external links

FIGURE 6.5: One of the lists of SocSciBot link analysis reports.

button. Once this calculation is complete, the network data are ready to be drawn by SocSciBot or loaded into a network analysis program like Pajek. To view the network in SocSciBot, click the (rather odd) report name *single.combined.full* to load the data into SocSciBot network. This network is initially displayed at random, but the domains can be moved to improve the readability of the diagram (e.g., placing interlinking sites close together and minimizing the crossing of lines). Alternatively, the Fruchterman–Reingold algorithm can be used to automatically arrange the sites, but the options panel settings for this algorithm (the *F-R* tab on the right of the screen) may need to be

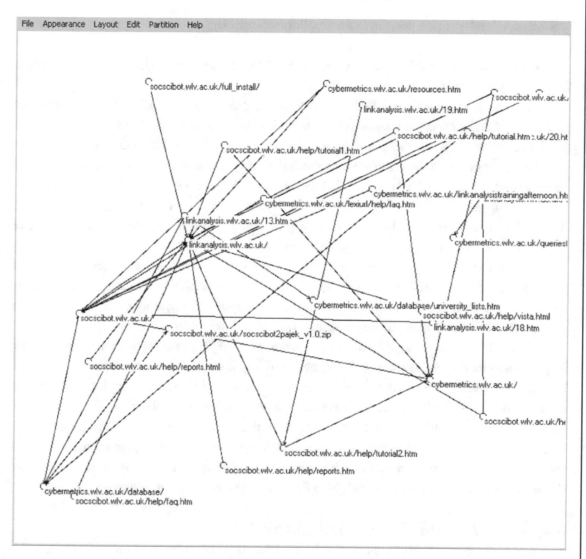

FIGURE 6.6: Interlinking pages in a SocSciBot Network diagram.

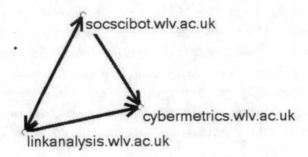

FIGURE 6.7: Interlinking domains in a SocSciBot Network diagram.

used to produce a reasonable result. See Section 5.4.1 (Rearranging, Saving, and Printing Network Diagrams) for more information.

    Step 8. Producing a site interlinking network diagram (Figure 6.6). To show links between sites rather than links between pages, several steps must be taken. In the SocSciBot Tools Main Reports screen, choose *Select types of links to include in reports* from the *Link Type Options* menu. Select the Domain aggregation level (rather than the default page aggregation level) and click OK. Now select again the *Network Diagram for Whole Project* tab and click on the *Re/Calculate Network* button. This will generate new data for a link diagram where the circles are domains rather than pages. To see this diagram, click on the report name *single.combined.full* again. As shown in Figure 6.7, all three domains contain pages that link to the other two domains.

    Note that network diagrams can be printed directly from the File/print menu item, but if a very high resolution version (e.g., 600 dpi) is needed for an academic publication, then a high-resolution document-producing printer driver must be installed first and then the diagram can be printed in high resolution via the print menu if the new printer driver is used.

    If anything goes wrong with the above operations, then please see the SocSciBot web site for help or post a report on the socscibot4.blogspot.com blog. If step 3 fails, however, because there are too many web sites or they must be crawled separately for some reason, then start a new project and do not select the multiple crawls option but enter instead the home page URL of the first site to be crawled. Select *crawl* to go to the main crawl screen, then select *Crawl Site* to start the crawl and then wait to be finished. For each site to be crawled, follow the same process, but make sure that all crawls are allocated to the same project. It is normally possible to run four crawls simultaneously on the same computer. Once all the crawls have finished, step 7 above can be followed.

6.4   OTHER USES FOR WEB CRAWLS

The data gathered by SocSciBot can also be used for other purposes than producing a network diagram. Below are some examples of uses:

- The impact of each web site created by links within the other web sites crawled can be seen in the link counts report. This is accessible via the Main Reports tab in the SocSciBot Tools Main Reports screen, and the information is in the ADM count summary report. This report contains the number of links to and from each site to and from each other site, as counted by page, directory, domain name, or web site.

- Network statistics are also available from the Main Reports tab in the SocSciBot Tools Main Reports screen. These include the total number of pages, directories, and domains linking between each pair of sites (the *from-to* reports). If more social network analysis statistics are needed, then the data matrix used to create the networks can be copied into a specialist program such as UCINET or extracted from Pajek.

- Network diagrams of individual sites can be produced but first the counting level must be changed to *pages* or *directories* rather than *sites* or *domains* in the example above (again using the Link Type Options menu) and the site self-links option should be checked in the same menu option box. Click on the *Network diagrams for individual sites* tab then click on the *Re/Calculate Network* button. Clicking on the domain name of a site will then produce a network diagram of the pages in the site in SocSciBot Network.

· · · ·

CHAPTER 7

Search Engines and Data Reliability

Commercial search engines are important for webometrics because they are used to supply the raw data for many studies, for example, via LexiURL Searcher. In addition, search engines are frequently investigated for the variability and coverage of their results because they are so widely used by web users to find information (Bar-Ilan, 2004). This chapter gives an overview of how search engines work and summarizes some webometric research about search engine reliability and coverage. The chapter is more theoretical and less directly practical than the preceding chapters but gives important background information to help understand and interpret the results of webometric techniques using commercial search engines.

7.1   SEARCH ENGINE ARCHITECTURE

The overall design or architecture of a search engine incorporates several components with completely different tasks. In essence, there are three main parts: the web crawler, the indexed page database, and the web page ranking engine (for a more complete characterization, see Brin & Page, 1998; Chakrabarti, 2003).

The web crawler has the task of finding web pages to populate its search engine's huge database. It does this by building a list of URLs of all known web pages and periodically visiting these pages to check for and download updated versions. When a page is downloaded, all hyperlinks within the page are extracted and added to the URL list, if they are not already there (Figure 7.1). In theory, the URL list may have begun life as a single URL or as a short list of URLs, but in any major search engine, it will contain billions of URLs.

The crawler's URL list does not contain the URL of every existing web page. This is because URLs are not added to it automatically when new web pages are created but only when the URL is submitted to the search engine (as occasionally happens) or when a link to the page is found by the crawler in a downloaded page. In consequence, entire web sites may not be found by a search engine because they are not linked to by other sites. A study in 1999 estimated that the search

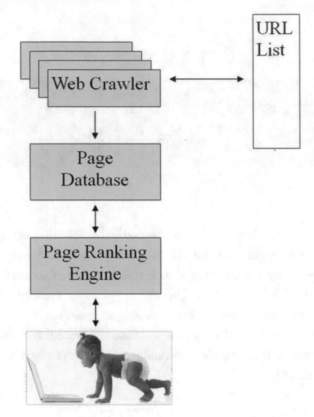

FIGURE 7.1: The three components of a commercial search engine that coordinate to get results to a web user.

engines of the day covered up to 17% of the web (Lawrence & Giles, 1999), a surprisingly low figure. The problem is exacerbated by pages that are password-protected, banned from crawling by their owners, or in a format that search engines cannot fully read or interpret (Java, Flash): the so-called invisible web (Sherman & Price, 2001). A consequence of this partial coverage for webometric studies is that *search engine results should never be interpreted as an accurate reflection of the web itself*.

The index of a search engine has the task of matching user queries to web pages in the search engine's database. It is able to use standard information retrieval techniques to do this efficiently, retrieving matching pages within tenths of a second from the billions in the database. Part of a search engine's algorithm may take shortcuts to return fast results, such as retrieving only 10% of the matching pages before creating the first page of results. In such a case, the algorithm may have to estimate the total number of matching pages in the remainder of the database to produce the hit count estimates displayed on the results pages. An additional complicating factor is that there may be multiple databases, perhaps with the most important or most frequently updated pages having their own areas. This can make the reported hit count estimates unreliable.

The page ranking engine is its most secret part of a commercial search engine. It uses information about the degree to which the matching pages appear to focus on the topic of the query, the importance or authority of the matching pages, and information about the user (e.g., their geographic location and search history) to rank the pages. The rank order is presumably designed to give the maximum chance that the user finds relevant information on the first results page so that they do not get frustrated and switch to a different search engine. Although the exact features used for ranking are not known for any major search engine, hyperlinks seem to be particularly useful as evidence of the importance of the target page. Google's key PageRank algorithm is based on the assumption that the most useful or important pages will tend to be linked too often and that links from high-quality pages are particularly good indicators of the value of target pages (Brin & Page, 1998). Newer algorithms like TrustRank can work in parallel with PageRank and seek to identify and reject pages that are likely to be spam because they are linked to by spam pages (Gyongyi, Garcia-Molina, & Pedersen, 2004).

7.1.1   Duplicate and Near-Duplicate Elimination

Duplicate and near-duplicate elimination is a factor that is important for webometrics in terms of understanding both the hit count estimates returned by search engines and the lists of URLs returned as matching a search.

In conjunction with ranking pages, search engines attempt to ensure that they do not return many similar or identical pages in their results (Gomes & Smith, 2003). This is because a page is unlikely to be relevant to a user if they have seen a similar page before and not visited it or have visited it but not found it useful. This duplicate and near-duplicate elimination seems to be done "just in time"—after ranking the results or as part of ranking the results—and can sometimes result in a drastic reduction in the total number of results delivered to the searcher. This is an important cause of unreliability in hit count estimates. One study of this phenomenon for Live Search suggested that large hit count estimates on the first results page (e.g., more than 8,000) would tend to reflect the number of URLs in the index matching the search, with little duplicate elimination. In contrast, small initial hit count estimates (e.g., less than 300) would tend to reflect the number of remaining URLs after all duplicate and near-duplicate elimination (Thelwall, 2008a). In-between figures and estimates on later results pages could reflect either or a combination of the two. This complicates the interpretation of hit count estimates in webometrics, especially when comparing large and small values.

Search engine duplicate elimination sometimes excludes multiple pages from the same site after the first two pages. It also seems to work based on page titles and the snippets about the pages displayed in the search engine results: if these are similar for two pages, then one of them might be eliminated. Because the snippets tend to be selected by the search engine to contain the search terms, this means that pages that are "locally similar" around the search terms may be regarded as essentially duplicates and held back from the user. Finally, because the duplicate elimination appears to occur in stages rather than all at once, it is possible to find near-duplicate results or multiple pages from the same site displayed on different results pages.

As a result of all the factors discussed above, the typical list of URLs returned by a search engine is likely to be incomplete with an unknown number of missing URLs. In addition, search engines return a maximum of 1,000 URLs per search. If a URL sample is taken from the search engine results, such as the first 10 matches, first 100 matches, or all 1,000 matches returned (if there are more than 1,000), then it is important to recognize that this is likely to be a biased sample because of the ranking mechanism. The results returned are probably the most authoritative pages, coming from the most important or authoritative sites, or the pages that match the searches best. Hence, *if URLs are to be processed to extract statistics, then it is best to use as large a list as possible to minimize bias.*

7.2   COMPARING DIFFERENT SEARCH ENGINES

The results returned by search engines for many searches can be very different from each other. These differences may be due to different ranking procedures, different coverage of the web by the crawlers, or different duplicate elimination processes (Thelwall, 2008c). Differing search engine results can be exploited for webometrics in two ways. First, statistics generated from results can be compared between search engines. This comparison can give an indication of how reliable the figures are. For example, if one search engine returned 90% of URLs from the .com domain but another returned 90% from the .edu domain, then this would cast doubt on both statistics. The second way of taking advantage of differences is to use multiple search engines and combine or average their results to minimize the idiosyncrasies of each.

7.3   RESEARCH INTO SEARCH ENGINE RESULTS

This section briefly describes a range of webometrics research into the performance of search engines in terms of the information returned. This introduces an important type of research and gives further background information about the reliability of search engine results.

Early research into search engines compared the hit count estimates over time and found them to vary significantly from day to day for many searches (Bar-Ilan, 1999). For example, the hit count estimates for the same search in a single search engine could fluctuate daily, with periodic step changes in results. Rousseau (1999) proposed a solution to this problem in the form of treating hit count estimates as a time series and using an average (or a moving average) for webometric investigations. Subsequent research found that the major search engines had become far more stable with their hit count estimates so that there did not seem to be a need for averaging any more (Thelwall, 2001b). Nevertheless, search engines did seem to periodically make substantial changes to their databases, such as increasing capacity, and so occasional variations still occurred.

A similar type of study investigated changes in hit count estimates between the different pages of results for the same search. It was found that the major three search engines at the time (Google, Yahoo, and Live Search) all reported changed hit count estimates on separate results pages occasionally, although these estimates did not vary frequently between pages. For example, a search might have a hit count estimate of 5,000 for the first seven results pages but 3,000 for the remaining 13 pages. About half of the sets of results pages had at least one change, and this change was almost always a downward revision. Overall, these findings suggested that duplicate elimination was the process driving the changes, and that this elimination was conducted periodically when delivering results but not for every page (Thelwall, 2008a).

Bar-Ilan has conducted a series of studies monitoring changes in the information reported by search engines over time. Picking the information science topic of informetrics (the study of information measurements), she ran searches in a range of search engines for this topic and compared the results from year to year. Although she found increasingly more results each year, she also discovered pages missing from the results: either pages apparently never found by a search engine's crawlers or pages previously known to a search engine but apparently subsequently forgotten (Bar-Ilan, 1999; Bar-Ilan & Peritz, 2004; Mettrop & Nieuwenhuysen, 2001). These forgotten pages could have been present in the search engine database but not returned to the searcher as a result of duplication, or they could have been discarded from the database for other reasons. Interestingly, Bar-Ilan was able to show that search engines sometimes did not return a page that matched the queries used even when the page was in the search engine's database and contained relevant information that was not in any other returned page. This latter point suggests that the near-duplicate elimination process is imperfect in terms of the contents of pages.

Vaughan, Cho, and others have researched the extent to which search engine results contain demonstrable biases. From the findings, it seems that search engines have clear but probably unintentional biases in favor of countries that were early adopters of the web but no language biases (Vaughan & Thelwall, 2004). The bias seems to be due to the link crawling process used by web crawlers to build their URL list of the web: newer web sites are less likely to be found because they are less likely to have been linked to by other web sites already known to the crawler. This is exacerbated by ranking algorithms, which have an age bias: search engines tend to rank older pages more highly than newer pages (Cho & Roy, 2004).

7.4 MODELING THE WEB'S LINK STRUCTURE

Some research in computer science and statistical physics has shed light on the link structure of the web, as covered by search engines. This gives additional background information about the web that is useful in interpreting the coverage of web crawlers and search engine ranking.

Research undertaken by the search engine AltaVista at the turn of the century analyzed interlinking between web pages within a single AltaVista web crawl and found that they could be split into five different chunks, as illustrated in Figure 7.2 (Broder et al., 2000). The core of the crawl was the "strongly connected component" (SCC). This is a huge collection of 28% of the pages that is particularly easily crawlable in the sense that a crawl starting at any SCC page would eventually reach the whole of the SCC. Hence, it seems reasonable to assume that all major search engines would have found virtually all of the SCC. "OUT" (21%) consists of all pages not in the SCC that are reachable by following links from the SCC. OUT is also very crawlable: a crawl starting in any SCC page would reach all OUT pages, but the reverse is not true: OUT pages do not form a good starting point for a crawl but should also be included almost entirely in any major search engine.

"IN" pages (21%) are those that are not in the SCC but from which the SCC can be reached by following links. IN pages are opposite to OUT: they do form a good starting point for a crawl because a crawl starting in IN will capture the whole SCC and out, as well as part of IN. No crawl starting point guarantees capturing much of IN, however, and so IN is likely to be only partly covered by other major search engines. The TENDRILS collection of pages (22%) is connected to IN,

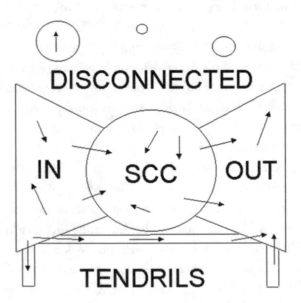

FIGURE 7.2: The link structure of an AltaVista web crawl (Broder et al., 2000).

OUT, or both in more exotic ways, and the DISCONNECTED pages (8%) are not connected in any way to the other components. Like IN, these last two components are unlikely to be well covered by other search engines.

The above discussion relates to the "topology" of the web. It reveals how there is likely to be a large core of the web that is well covered by all search engines and that the rest of the web is likely to be covered unevenly.

A second type of research has focused on identifying mathematical laws in link count data. This has helped to popularize terms like *long tail* and *power law*. The main finding is that link counts are extremely unevenly distributed between pages. Although most web pages attract only a few links or no links at all, a small number attract millions. In fact, the number of links to web pages approximately follows a mathematical relationship known as a power law. Figure 7.3 gives

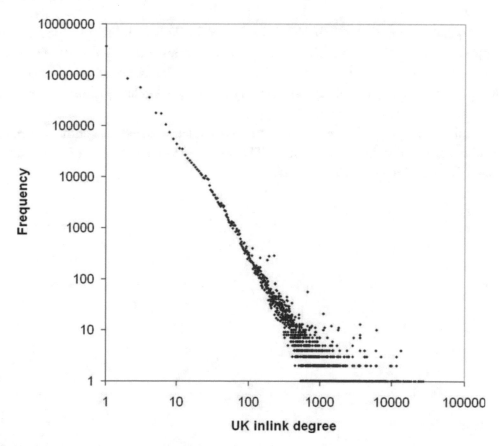

FIGURE 7.3: The power-law distribution of links to U.K. academic web sites (Thelwall & Wilkinson, 2003).

an example of its shape for links to U.K. university web sites from other U.K. university web sites. Note that the axes of this graph are logarithmic, which hides the extent to which pages that have attracted only a few links are enormously more common than pages that have attracted many links. For example, pages with 10 inlinks are about 500 times common than pages with 100 inlinks.

Power laws tend to arise when a "rich get richer" phenomenon is at work. This suggests that web pages tend to attract new links partly because they already have some links (Barabási & Albert, 1999). In fact, the more inlinks that a page has, the more new inlinks it is likely to attract. This can be explained by search engine ranking. Pages that have already attracted many inlinks are likely to be near the top of search engine results and so are easily found. Other factors being equal, these will be the best known pages and the most likely to attract any new links created. As mentioned above, a consequence of this is that it is difficult for new sites to get noticed because they start with no links and hence are at a disadvantage compared to established sites that have already attracted many links.

Although the power law rule holds approximately for the web in general, it does not necessarily apply to specific collections of single types of pages. For instance, it is a poor fit for university home pages (Pennock, Flake, Lawrence, Glover, & Giles, 2002). For small groups of pages of a similar type, it may be that organizational factors such as size and industry sector are more important than the rich-get-richer phenomenon.

A statistical property of power laws relevant to webometrics is that their arithmetic means are not useful because of the skewed distribution. The median is a better measure of central tendency because it effectively ignores the huge values.

•   •   •   •

CHAPTER 8

Tracking User Actions Online

This chapter gives a brief introduction to methods for tracking user actions online that do not rely on data collected from search engines or web crawlers. This is webometrics in the sense of analyzing web data quantitatively, although the raw data used are not derived from web pages but from other sources of information about how web pages are accessed. For more information, see a review article about web metrics (Heinonen & Hägert, 2004), the computer science web usage mining field (Srivastava, Cooley, Deshpande, & Tan, 2000), and special information science user-tracking topics such as deep log analysis (Huntington, Nicholas, & Jamali, 2007) and log analysis for scientific impact measurement (Brody, Harnad, & Carr, 2006; Moed, 2005).

8.1   SINGLE-SITE WEB ANALYTICS AND LOG FILE ANALYSIS

The most common method of evaluating the impact of a web site or analyzing the activities of visitors to a web site is web log file analysis. Web server log files typically contain detailed information about the page accesses of a web site's visitors. These files are created by the web server program that operates the site or by third-party programs like Google Analytics if the web site owner places appropriate code in each page. In either case, the raw data files typically contain information revealing the pages each user visited, which web site directed them to the site, the approximate length of time spent on the site, and the approximate geographic location of the visitors. Web analytics software, sometimes called web server log file analysis software, can process this information to report useful summary statistics, such as the daily, weekly, or monthly total number of unique visitors; most common web sources of new visitors to the site; and most popular pages within the site. This is gives an overall impression of how the site is being used and how this usage is changing over time. For example, the Google Analytics program surprisingly revealed that the most popular page within Link Analysis web site linkanalysis.wlv.ac.uk was the page supporting chapter 23 (see Figure 8.1), and delving deeper into the report revealed that the most common source of visitors for that page was a Wikipedia article about networks.

The knowledge of which web site a user visited previously gives useful information about which sites link to the site analyzed and how much traffic these source sites send. If the source site is

FIGURE 8.1: Detail from the Google Analytics report for linkanalysis.wlv.ac.uk showing the geographic origins of visitors (top) and the most commonly visited page (bottom).

a search engine like Google, then the previous page will be a search results page and the URL of this results page encodes within it the original search terms. As a result, web analytics software is able to report the search terms that led users to a site, which gives useful insights into *why* they visited it.

Web analytics information is more detailed and more robust than the equivalent information from link impact reports. For example, the most popular pages in a web site could be estimated in a link impact report by finding which pages were most commonly targeted by links from other web sites, whereas the web log files would contain accurate visitor statistics. Nevertheless, web analytics are typically unsuitable for an impact evaluation because they can only be applied with the permission of web site owners so they cannot be used to demonstrate impact relative to similar or competitor sites. If possible, both should be used together for any site as the information that they give is complementary, although it partly overlaps.

8.2   MULTIPLE-SITE WEB ANALYTICS

A number of companies track the activities of large numbers of web users, either through a program installed on user computers or through access to anonymized activity logs by arrangement with individual Internet service providers. Three currently prominent such companies are HitWise, Comscore, and Alexa. These give out some information free in the form of press releases or web reports but earn revenue by selling more comprehensive data. Alexa regularly lists the most visited web sites in the world and in individual countries. This is useful to track and confirm the importance of rapidly emerging web sites.

A book written by HitWise provides many examples of the kinds of insights that this kind of data can give into online human behavior (Trancer, 2008). One of the more impressive conclusions was that increased activity in social network sites coincided with reduced visits to pornographic sites. It seems that significant numbers of web users were using social network sites instead of pornography or during times previously occupied by pornography use. A similar analysis showed that generic gambling like poker was connected to major sporting events because a proportion of gamblers would use online gaming sites when sports betting was unavailable.

Web usage data would be ideal for online analytics reports because it contains the same kind of information about web sites as server log files but would include data about competitors' web sites. Unfortunately, however, it is likely to be expensive to purchase and thus impractical for most purposes. For relatively popular sites, it might be possible to use Alexa's free webmaster web traffic statistics (see www.alexa.com and sign up), which would give valuable additional statistics.

8.3   SEARCH ENGINE LOG FILE ANALYSIS

The log files of commercial search engines contain a record of all user searches and can be used by the search engines to find out things like the most popular search terms, which links tend to be clicked in response to given keyword searches, and how many results pages tend to be viewed before users give up. This information is normally private, although some has been released to selected researchers and search engines sometimes make public some summary data, such as the most popular search terms or the fastest increasing search terms (e.g., www.google.com/trends/hottrends). In addition, users can produce time series trend graphs of reasonably popular search terms through Google Trends (www.google.com/trends).

The results of search engine log file analysis have been written up extensively elsewhere, most notably in a book (Spink & Jansen, 2004), but some key results can be summarized here (based on data from Excite, AltaVista, and AllTheWeb). Searchers tend to submit simple searches with an average of about 2.5 keywords per query, although this average seems to be slowly increasing and searchers reasonably often construct some kind of complex query (about a quarter of the time), such as a phrase search or one involving Boolean operators. Approximately three quarters of searches stop at the first results page, showing the importance of the top search results.

. . . . .

CHAPTER 9

Advanced Techniques

This chapter contains a selection of advanced webometrics techniques. Some are extensions or applications of the topics in previous chapters but others are new.

9.1 QUERY SPLITTING

The major search engines return a maximum of 1,000 results for any query. This means that if you submit a search and keep clicking on the "Next Page" link to see more results, then the results will stop when about 1,000 have been displayed. This limit is a problem for webometric techniques like web impact reports and link impact reports, which rely on lists of URLs and may be compromised if significantly incomplete lists are returned.

Query splitting is a technique to get additional URLs matching a search beyond the maximum of 1,000 normally returned (Thelwall, 2008a). The idea is simple: submit a set of modified versions of the original query and then combine the results of each modified version. This works as long as any result that matches a modified query also matches the original one. This matching can be ensured by always starting with the original query and modifying it by adding extra terms. For example, suppose that the query *jaguar* returns the maximum 1,000 URLs, but Google reports that there are about 1 million matching pages. To get additional matches, new queries could be made like *jaguar animal* or *jaguar car*. Any result that matched either of these would contain the word jaguar and would therefore match the original search. The chances are that some of the 1,000 URLs matching each of the two searches above would not be the same as the results returned for the original search and so combining the results of all three is likely to give many more than 1,000 URLs, and up to a maximum of 3,000 URLs, all of which match the original search.

Although the above method could be applied with a human selecting the terms to add, it is also possible to automate it using automatically submitted queries. For example, the query splitting technique selects a term that occurs in about 10% of the titles and snippets of the first 1,000 results and makes two queries: one adding this term to the original query and the other subtracting it. Suppose that the 10% word chosen for the query *jaguar* was *cat*. Then the two new queries would *jaguar cat* and *jaguar −cat*. An advantage of this process is that the two new queries cannot have any URLs in common and so if both return 1,000 results then this would give 2,000 different URLs in total. This query splitting can be repeated again on the two new searches to give up to 4,000 new URLs. For instance, suppose that the 10% word for *jaguar cat* was *tiger*. Then, the two new queries would be *jaguar cat tiger* and *jaguar cat −tiger*. Similarly, for the query *jaguar-cat*, suppose that the 10% word was *engine*. Then, the two new queries would be *jaguar −cat engine* and *jaguar −cat −engine*. Figure 9.1 gives an additional case.

In theory, the query splitting process could be repeated until all searches returned less than 1,000 matches, but in practice, search engines have limits on the complexity of searches processed (e.g., a maximum of 10 terms or 150 characters per search) and so this is not always possible. If it is possible, then the final set of queries should in theory give all results known to the search engine, but this is not likely to be the case because of issues related to duplicate elimination in the results (see Section 7.1.1, Duplicate and Near-Duplicate Elimination). Hence the final results set should be made by combining all results, including those from the original query and from all intermediate steps. Even this combined list is unlikely to be exhaustive, however.

The query splitting technique described above is available in LexiURL Searcher professional for researchers but is not in the online version. This is because query splitting is quite powerful in terms of generating many searches and hence it is restricted to avoid accidental overuse. A simple alternative is to manually select a few splitting terms or to split by searching separately for each TLD. For example, in the latter case to search for Jaguar, the first three searches might be *jaguar site:com*, *jaguar site:edu* and *jaguar site:org*.

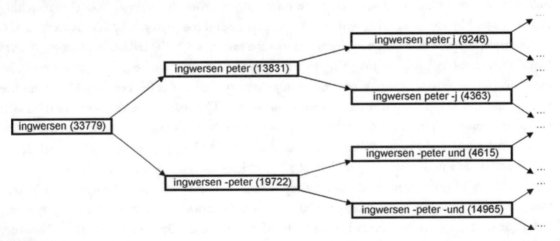

FIGURE 9.1: An illustration of the start of query splitting for the query "Ingwersen." The number of matches for each query is in brackets (Thelwall, 2008a).

9.2   VIRTUAL MEMETICS

Virtual memetics is a set of methods to track online the evolution over time of a single meme, that is, a single transmitted unit of cultural information. The method was developed to track the international online spread and morphing of a joke but is applicable to any text-based information that is widely circulated via the web (Shifman & Thelwall, submitted for publication). It is based on analyzing a sample of relevant web pages and using date-specific searches to track evolution over time.

The first step of virtual memetics is common to many webometrics methods: constructing an appropriate search engine query to match pages containing the meme (e.g., a joke) and building a list of URLs or matching pages either via an automatic query submission program like LexiURL Searcher or using manual searches. Query splitting (see the section on this) may be needed if there are more results than the maximum 1,000 returned by a search engine.

The second step is to download a random sample of a manageable collection of web pages from the list (e.g., 300) with a maximum of one page per site.

The third step is to automatically or manually analyze the sample for variations in the meme. The idea behind this is to capture key variations in the meme made by individuals as it circulates. Whereas automatic methods might include clustering by text similarity, the manual method would essentially be a human clustering by similarity. Ultimately, however, unless the statistical clustering results are particularly clear-cut, it will be a human decision to distinguish between relatively minor meme variations and more substantial variations that deserve to be named and analyzed as a whole. For example, in the initial study using this technique, there were joke variations labeled sexist, feminist, and Indian, among others.

The fourth step is to track the evolution over time of the variations by identifying evidence about their earliest appearance online. This cannot be perfectly achieved because email cannot be tracked over time and web pages disappear, but there are three different methods that can jointly be used to give an indication of when a meme or meme variation first occurred. Google blog search results can be sorted by date, so one useful statistic that can easily be obtained is the earliest date in which the meme variation appeared in a blog post indexed by Google blog search (blogsearch. google.com). Similarly, a Google Groups search (groups.google.com) can be used to identify the earliest occurrence of each variation in a Google group. There are many other similar search services, but these often have a time limitation of 6 or 12 months and so they may not be useful. A final method is to use AltaVista's date-specific search (available in the advanced search section of www.altavista.com). This allows searches for web pages indexed by AltaVista that are older than a given date and have not been modified since that date. Putting together these three methods, the estimated creation date would be the earliest of the three dates. This cross-checking does not give

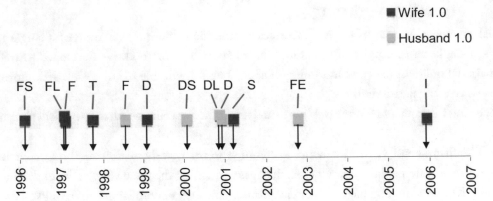

FIGURE 9.2: A timeline of the earliest appearances of major variations of two memes online extracted using the virtual memetics method. Each code represents a different major variation (e.g., FE is the feminist variant) (Shifman & Thelwall, submitted for publication).

a guarantee that the date is correct but seems like a reasonable method to produce an approximation. The end result of the steps so far would produce a timeline of the major meme variations and their estimated dates of emergence. Figure 9.2 gives an example of a timeline obtained from this method.

A fifth and optional step is to identify and track translations of the meme and meme variations. This can be achieved using steps 1–4 above on translations of the jokes. In addition, for extra coverage of non-English languages, it may be useful to also search for additional matches with language-specific or regional search engines or interfaces for the major search engines. Finally, comparing the variations of the meme in its original language with its translated international variations may reveal key international similarities or variations.

9.3 WEB ISSUE ANALYSIS

Web issue analysis (Thelwall, Vann, & Fairclough, 2006) is the tracking of the spread of an issue online. For example, one study attempted to identify all online mentions of the United Nations Integrated Water Resources Management concept to discover how international it had become. The methods of issue analysis start with those for a web impact assessment but also include some additional linguistic techniques. Hence, a web issue analysis is based on one or more web searches for the issue, with matching URLs or web sites counted and a content analysis conducted to validate and help interpret the results, and a TLD breakdown used to suggest the international spread of the topic.

The additional linguistic method that makes web issue analysis different from web impact assessment is the identification of words that occur relatively often in web pages mentioning the

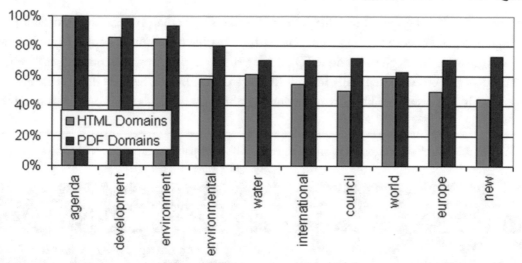

FIGURE 9.3: Most common nouns in Integrated Water Resources Management web pages, as measured by the percentage of domains (Thelwall et al., 2006).

issue. This can be useful to identify concepts that may have been missed by the content analysis. Word counting for this purpose is impractically time-consuming and so it can only be done with the support of a text analysis computer program (e.g., the text analysis component of SocSciBot). In addition, a control group collection of texts should be similarly analyzed so that a comparison of the two results can identify words that are relatively more common in the issue-relevant pages. This then produces two lists of words and word frequencies: one for issue-mentioning pages and one for the control group. These two can be compared by identifying relatively highly ranked words in the issue-specific list or by using formal statistical methods to identify unusually high frequency words in the issue-specific list (McEnery & Wilson, 2001; Thelwall et al., 2006). An alternative method is to use natural language processing techniques to extract nouns and noun phrases from the matching web pages, reporting the most common of these. Figure 9.3 illustrates the results of this for a web issue analysis.

9.4 DATA MINING SOCIAL NETWORK SITES

Some quantitative studies of the web have focused on specific web sites or types of web site, using specially designed programs to extract detailed information from each page, beyond just the links extracted by web crawlers. This section attempts to mine public information from the social network site MySpace, using modified web crawlers.

MySpace became apparently the most popular social network site in the world in 2006 but was subsequently overtaken by Facebook in mid-2008. It is particularly suitable for detailed webometric analysis because the profile pages of members older than 16 years are by default public, although users can choose to make them private. It is possible to randomly sample MySpace members because each one is given a unique ID number, these numbers are given out consecutively, and the numbers can be converted easily into profile page URLs. In fact, because the IDs are given out consecutively, it is even possible to use a random number generator to sample people who joined on

TABLE 9.1: A classification by profile owner of U.K. MySpace swearing types (427 swear words) (Thelwall, 2008b).

LINGUISTIC TYPE	M F	EXAMPLES (SLASHES // SEPARATE COMMENTS)
Predicative -*ve* adjective	0% 1%	...and your myspace page is fucked
Cursing expletive	1% 3%	so fuck you jim bob! X // bollocks to this
Destinational usage	3% 1%	fuck....right....off.... // Chris you're slacking again !!! Get the fuck off myspace lol !!
Emphatic adverb/adjective OR adverbial booster OR premodifying intensifying negative adjective	32% 38%	and we r guna go to town again n make a ryt fuckin nyt of it again lol // see look i'm fucking commenting u back // lol and stop fucking tickleing me!! // Thanks for the party last night it was fucking good and you are great hosts.
General expletive	6% 7%	fuck i didnt know this was u lol // lol.....nooooo waaaayyyyyy....fuck !!!
Idiomatic set phrase OR figurative extension of literal meaning	28% 17%	think am gonna get him an album or summet fuck nows // qu'est ce que fuck? // what the fuck pubehead whos pete and why is this necicery mate
Literal usage denoting taboo referent	3% 3%	Oh n shaggin dead people // ...that does not mean I am the village yokal idiot or that daddy fucked me with a rusty broken pitch fork...
Pronominal with undefined referent	0% 1%	Occupation: No.1 Cunt Kicker-inner.
Personal insult to defined entity	27% 28%	i m such a sleep deprived twat alot of the time! // 3rd? i thought i was your main man [] Fucker

any given date. Several studies have taken advantage of the public nature of many MySpace profiles to automatically extract detailed information from them (Hinduja & Patchin, 2008; Liu, 2007).

One early study focused on the proximity of online MySpace Friends by taking a person's "Friends" and attempting to extract detailed information about their location from the relevant profile section. Initial results suggested that most Friends tended to live close together, for example, in the same town (Escher, 2007). Another study took random members and paired them with random MySpace Friends from their Friend lists, and compared their reported attributes and beliefs. The results showed that similar people tended to be Friends disproportionately often, including for similarity in terms of age, religion, country of residence, and ethnicity. In contrast, and despite most offline studies of friendship, members were not disproportionately often Friends with others of the same sex (Thelwall, 2009). This study only considered active Friendship in the sense of commenting on Friends' profiles. A related study investigated swearing in the comments written on Friends' profiles, finding again, in contrast to previous offline studies, that strong swearing was equally prevalent in the profiles of male and female U.K. members. In the United States, however, strong swearing was more common in male profiles. In both cases, swearing occurred in most profiles and was particularly prevalent in younger members' profiles. Table 9.1 gives an example of the many linguistic types of swearing found. This is interesting because informal friendly swearing is rarely written down, and hence, MySpace gives an almost unique opportunity to study swearing on a large scale (Thelwall, 2008b).

The techniques discussed above are different from most webometrics research in that they rely on data mining within the text of the web pages—that is, extracting specific facts from the pages. This requires specially customized programs, which is another difference from most webometrics research. There are many other examples of projects that also extract information from web pages to address research questions. For example, one attempted to automatically detect web page genres from their contents (Rehm, 2002).

9.5   SOCIAL NETWORK ANALYSIS AND SMALL WORLDS

The webometric techniques that generate networks lend themselves to analysis by any one of the many academic network analysis techniques, whether from math (e.g., graph theory), physics (e.g., complex network theory), or the social sciences (e.g., social network analysis). This section discusses the last of these, that most relevant to typical social sciences research.

Social network analysis (Wasserman & Faust, 1994) is a research field concerned with the analysis of networks of individuals or organizations. Its principal belief is that some social systems cannot be properly understood when analyzed at the level of individual components but are better analyzed as networks of interacting parts. A classic example is communication within a primitive village environment: to find out how information travels, it is necessary to know about each person's friends and acquaintances and their talking patterns. Social network analysis has developed a range of metrics for assessing various aspects of a network. Some of these metrics are centered on individual network nodes: for example, the *degree centrality* of each person in a village might be defined to be the number of friends that they have. Other metrics are based more on the structure of a network as a whole. For instance, the *betweenness centrality* of a node is the probability that a random path between two random nodes will pass through the given node. This is high for nodes that play an important bridging function—they may not have many connections, but they are important for communication.

Social network analysis can be applied to collections of web pages or web sites with the nodes in the social network being the web pages or web sites and the connection between them being the hyperlinks. The metrics of social network analysis are potentially useful to describe network properties and to help compare networks, but caution should be exercised when applying them to web networks because the assumptions made when defining them—typically that the connections between nodes are the key channels of communication—do not necessarily apply to the web. For example, although hyperlinks can be used to travel between web sites, it is probably more common to switch between sites via a bookmark or a search engine search. Blogspace and discussion forums could well be exceptions to this, however.

One interesting application of social network analysis techniques on the web is Lennart Björneborn's analysis of cross-topic connectors in the U.K. academic web space (Björneborn, 2004, 2006). He found that although most links between academic web sites in different universities connected similar research areas, some were interdisciplinary connectors. Computer science web sites were particularly prominent in forming such cross-topic connections.

9.6 FOLKSONOMY TAGGING

The tags generated by users of Web 2.0 content-based systems like YouTube, Flickr, and del.icio.us have generated much research because they are a new and relatively unfettered method of describing resources that may help information retrieval (Golder & Huberman, 2006). Webometrics research can contribute to the understanding of this informal "folksonomy" tagging by identifying common tags and types of tags. For instance, one study extracted tags from millions of YouTube, Flickr, and del.icio.us pages to find the most frequent tags in each system (Ding, Toma, Kang, Fried, & Yan, 2008). The differences in the results were evidence of significant variations in the way that users used the tagging facilities.

9.7 API PROGRAMMING AND MASHUPS

As discussed in other chapters, applications programming interfaces (APIs) are pathways provided by search engines and some other software to give programmers simple access to useful facilities, subject to certain restrictions such as daily usage limits (Mayr & Tosques, 2005). By early 2009, APIs of potential use in webometrics were provided by Yahoo, Live Search, Google (only for existing users), Technorati, and Flickr, among others. Given access to programming skills or a program like LexiURL Searcher that can tap into the relevant API, this gives webometrics researchers potential access to large amounts of data.

APIs are typically configured to allow a program to submit a specific request for information in a standard format. For example, the Yahoo API allows searches to be submitted together with a range of parameters, such as the number of results to return (up to 50). This request must be encoded and submitted as a URL in a format specified in the Yahoo API instructions. The information returned by the Yahoo API in response to this request is structured in an XML document format described in the API documentation. This document can be easily processed by a computer program to extract the desired information.

Most webometrics research using search engines has used APIs to allow a large amount of data to be analyzed without requiring extensive human labor. An example of webometrics API-based research that is different to the topics discussed in this book is a study of Flickr that used the Flickr API to randomly select pictures from a Flickr Group for a subsequent human content analysis (Angus, Thelwall, & Stuart, 2008).

Although currently rare in webometrics research, API functionality can be extended through combining different sources of data to produce a *mashup*. This is a program that operates online via multiple data sources or APIs. An example of mashup research is Tobias Escher's combination of MySpace data with Google Maps to chart the positions of all of a MySpace member's friends (Escher, 2007), as discussed above.

· · · ·

CHAPTER 10

Summary and Future Directions

This book introduces a set of webometrics methods that should be widely useful in the social sciences and information science in particular. *Blog searching* can identify fluctuations in public interest in a topic as well as reveal the causes of these fluctuations. This can be supported by Google search volume data to check that any trends found are not peculiar to blogs. *Link impact analysis* can be used to indicate the impact of web sites or pages, and *web impact assessment* can be used to indicate the online impact of sets of documents or terms. In addition, *hyperlink-based network diagrams* can be used to identify patterns of interlinking between sets of web sites. All of these techniques are relatively simple to apply, and can be used as one of a number of methods to investigate a research problem or can be applied in a more in-depth manner as a separate research method. The techniques can also be applied to investigate online phenomena or the online reflections of offline phenomena. All of the methods have a number of limitations, however, that mean that their results should be interpreted carefully and cautiously in many cases.

In addition to discussing the above webometric techniques, this book also discusses tools to carry out the studies (blog search engines, SocSciBot, and LexiURL Searcher) and gives practical instructions for using them. A range of supporting background information is also given, such as on the workings of search engines, to help interpret the research. An important topic for webometrics is the reliability of search engines, and this is a separate area of study within webometrics. Finally, the book gives a brief introduction into a range of advanced webometric topics that have more specific purposes than the main techniques discussed.

The future of webometrics seems to lie in finding new applications of the established techniques and to develop new methods in response to the emergence of new information sources. This is partly reliant on the provision of free search interfaces (e.g., Alexa traffic ranking, the BlogPulse search engine) by companies that have the resources to collect data on a large scale. Such interfaces help to make the techniques easily accessible to the wider research community. Moreover, webometrics research is likely to continue to develop parallel data collection and analysis software, such as SocSciBot, that are not dependent on free data sources.

In terms of research topics, tagging has emerged as an important new research area (i.e., the study of the keywords assigned to online resources by users), although one that is of primary relevance to information science and computer science rather than the wider social sciences. It may be also possible to extend current social network research, but this is dependent on the privacy models of sites being sufficiently open to allow webometrics research. As of early 2009, MySpace was the only major social network site that allowed webometrics research, so the future of this kind of study is tenuous.

An important indication that webometrics is likely to continue to expand in the future is the apparently irrevocable establishment of user-generated content as an important part of the Internet. It seems inevitable that some of the future big online applications or movements will include the generation of data in a form that could be counted and analyzed to generate public opinion or other trends. This will allow social scientists to continue to gain new insights into both online and offline phenomena.

More information related to this book and an opportunity to comment is at webometrics .wlv.ac.uk.

• • • •

Glossary

Colink   Either a co-inlink or a co-outlink. The term *colink* is sometimes used when it is clear from the context whether it is a co-inlink or a co-outlink.

Co-inlink, co-inlinked   Two web sites that are both linked to by a third web site are called co-inlinked. In practice, co-inlinks are often derived from search engine data and in this case an additional restriction applies: two co-inlinked pages are always linked from a single co-inlinked page in a third web site.

Co-outlink, co-outlinked   Two web sites that both link to a third web site are said to co-outlink. In practice, co-outlinks are often derived from search engine data and in this case an additional restriction applies: two co-outlinking pages always link to a single page in a third web site.

Direct link   A hyperlink from one web page to another.

Directory or URL directory   Any URL ending in a slash (e.g., http://www.wlv.ac.uk/admin/).

Domain or domain name   The part of a typical URL following the initial http:// and preceding the next slash, if any (e.g., www.microsoft.com, www.wlv.ac.uk).

Domain inlink/outlink   see inlink/outlink.

Duplicate elimination and near-duplicate elimination   In the context of search engines, this is the phenomenon that causes search engines to hold back some of the pages matching a user's query because pages previously returned appear to be similar. This similarity appears to be based on either the pages appearing in the same web site or the titles and snippets from the pages appearing in the results being quite similar.

Hit count estimate   The figure reported on results pages by search engines as the total number of matching pages. For example, the 10,000 in "Results 1–10 of about 10,000" is the hit count estimate from a Google search.

Inlink   A hyperlink to a web page from another web page, sometimes called a page inlink. A site inlink is a link to a page from a page in a different web site. Similarly, a domain inlink is a link to a page from a page with a different domain name. The term *inlink* is sometimes used when it is clear from the context whether it is a page, domain, or site inlink.

Interlinking   Two web pages interlink if either one has a link to the other. Similarly, two web sites or domains interlink if any page in one has a link to any page in another.

Outlink   A hyperlink from a page to a different web page, sometimes called a page outlink. A site outlink is an outlink from a page to a page within a different web site. Similarly, a domain outlink is a link from a page to a page with a different domain name. The *term* outlink is sometimes used when it is clear from the context whether it is a page, domain, or site outlink.

Page inlink/outlink, see inlink/outlink.

Site inlink/outlink, see inlink/outlink.

STLD   The last two segments of a domain name after the penultimate dot if a standard naming system is used (e.g., com.au, org.uk, ac.nz), otherwise the TLD of the domain name.

TLD   Top-level domain. The last segment of a domain name after the final dot (e.g., com, org, uk, cn, jp, de, dk, fi, ca, edu).

Web site   A loose term that at its most general encompasses any collection of web pages that form a coherent whole in terms of content or owning organization. In webometrics, the term is also used for all collections of web pages sharing the same domain name ending, where this ending includes one dot-separated segment immediately preceding the STLD (e.g., wlv.ac.uk, microsoft.com).

References

Adamic, L., & Glance, N. (2005). The political blogosphere and the 2004 US election: Divided they blog. *WWW2005 blog workshop*, retrieved May 5, 2006, from http://www.blogpulse.com/papers/2005/AdamicGlanceBlogWWW.pdf.

Aguillo, I. F., Granadino, B., Ortega, J. L., & Prieto, J. A. (2006). Scientific research activity and communication measured with cybermetrics indicators. *Journal of the American Society for Information Science and Technology, 57*(10), pp. 1296–1302. doi:10.1002/asi.20433

Almind, T. C., & Ingwersen, P. (1997). Informetric analyses on the World Wide Web: Methodological approaches to 'Webometrics'. *Journal of Documentation, 53*(4), pp. 404–426. doi:10.1108/EUM0000000007205

Angus, E., Thelwall, M., & Stuart, D. (2008). General patterns of tag usage amongst university groups in Flickr. *Online Information Review, 32*(1), pp. 89–101.

Barabási, A. L., & Albert, R. (1999). Emergence of scaling in random networks. *Science, 286*(5439), pp. 509–512.

Bar-Ilan, J. (1999). *Search engine results over time—a case study on search engine stability*, retrieved January 26, 2006, from http://www.cindoc.csic.es/cybermetrics/articles/v2i1p1.html.

Bar-Ilan, J. (2004). The use of Web search engines in information science research. *Annual Review of Information Science and Technology, 38*, pp. 231–288. doi:10.1002/aris.1440380106

Bar-Ilan, J., & Peritz, B. C. (2004). Evolution, continuity, and disappearance of documents on a specific topic on the Web: A longitudinal study of 'informetrics'. *Journal of the American Society for Information Science and Technology, 55*(11), pp. 980–990. doi:10.1002/asi.20049

Barjak, F., & Thelwall, M. (2008). A statistical analysis of the web presences of European life sciences research teams. *Journal of the American Society for Information Science and Technology, 59*(4), pp. 628–643. doi:10.1002/asi.20776

Björneborn, L. (2004). *Small-world link structures across an academic web space—a library and information science approach*. Royal School of Library and Information Science, Copenhagen, Denmark.

Björneborn, L. (2006). 'Mini small worlds' of shortest link paths crossing domain boundaries in an academic Web space. *Scientometrics, 68*(3), pp. 395–414. doi:10.1007/s11192-006-0119-8

Björneborn, L., & Ingwersen, P. (2004). Toward a basic framework for webometrics. *Journal of the American Society for Information Science and Technology, 55*(14), pp. 1216–1227. doi:10.1002/asi.20077

Borgman, C. L., & Furner, J. (2002). Scholarly communication and bibliometrics. *Annual Review of Information Science and Technology, 36*, pp. 3–72. doi:10.1002/aris.1440360102

Börner, K., Sanyal, S., & Vespignani, A. (2007). Network science. *Annual Review of Information Science and Technology, 41*, pp. 537–607. doi:10.1002/aris.2007.1440410119

Boyd, D., & Ellison, N. (2007). Social network sites: Definition, history, and scholarship. *Journal of Computer-Mediated Communication, 13*(1), retrieved December 10, 2007, from http://jcmc .indiana.edu/vol2013/issue2001/boyd.ellison.html.

Brin, S., & Page, L. (1998). The anatomy of a large scale hypertextual Web search engine. *Computer Networks and ISDN Systems, 30*(1–7), pp. 107–117. doi:10.1016/S0169-7552(98)00110-X

Broder, A., Kumar, R., Maghoul, F., Raghavan, P., Rajagopalan, S., Stata, R., et al. (2000). Graph structure in the web. *Journal of Computer Networks, 33*(1–6), pp. 309–320. doi:10.1016/S1389-1286(00)00083-9

Brody, T., Harnad, S., & Carr, L. (2006). Earlier Web usage statistics as predictors of later citation impact. *Journal of the American Society for Information Science and Technology, 57*(8), pp. 1060–1072. doi:10.1002/asi.20373

Chakrabarti, S. (2003). *Mining the Web: Analysis of hypertext and semi structured data.* New York: Morgan Kaufmann.

Chakrabarti, S., Joshi, M. M., Punera, K., & Pennock, D. M. (2002). *The structure of broad topics on the Web,* from http://www2002.org/CDROM/refereed/338.

Chen, C. (2004). *Information visualization: Beyond the horizon, 2nd ed.* New York: Springer.

Cho, J., & Roy, S. (2004). Impact of Web search engines on page popularity. *Proceedings of the World-Wide Web Conference, May 2004,* retrieved February 4, 2007, from http://oak.cs.ucla .edu/~cho/papers/cho-bias.pdf.

Crane, D. (1972). *Invisible colleges: Diffusion of knowledge in scientific communities.* London: University of Chicago Press.

Cronin, B., Snyder, H. W., Rosenbaum, H., Martinson, A., & Callahan, E. (1998). Invoked on the web. *Journal of the American Society for Information Science, 49*(14), pp. 1319–1328. doi:10.1002/(SICI)1097-4571(1998)49:14<1319::AID-ASI9>3.0.CO;2-W

Ding, W., & Marchionini, G. (1996). A comparative study of web search service performance. *Proceedings of the 59th Annual Meeting of the American Society for Information Science, Baltimore, M.D.,* pp. 136–142.

Ding, Y., Toma, I., Kang, S. J., Fried, M., & Yan, Z. (2008). Data mediation and interoperation in social Web: Modeling, crawling and integrating social tagging data. *Workshop on Social Web Search and Mining (WWW2008)*, retrieved October 20, 2008, from http://keg.cs.tsinghua .edu.cn/SWSM2008/short%2020papers/swsm2008_submission_2005.pdf.

Escher, T. (2007). The geography of (online) social networks. *Web 2.0, York University*, retrieved September 18, 2007, from http://people.oii.ox.ac.uk/escher/wp-content/uploads/2007/2009/ Escher_York_presentation.pdf.

Flake, G. W., Lawrence, S., Giles, C. L., & Coetzee, F. M. (2002). Self-organization and identification of Web communities. *IEEE Computer, 35*, pp. 66–71. doi:10.1109/2.989932

Foot, K., & Schneider, S. (2006). *Web campaigning*. Cambridge, MA: MIT Press.

Foot, K. A., & Schneider, S. M. (2002). Online action in campaign 2000: An exploratory analysis of the U.S. political web sphere. *Journal of Broadcasting and Electronic Media, 46*(2), pp. 222–244. doi:10.1207/s15506878jobem4602_4

Foot, K. A., Schneider, S. M., Dougherty, M., Xenos, M., & Larsen, E. (2003). Analyzing linking practices: Candidate sites in the 2002 US electoral web sphere. *Journal of Computer Mediated Communication, 8*(4), from http://www.ascusc.org/jcmc/vol8/issue4/foot.html.

Fruchterman, T. M. J., & Reingold, E. M. (1991). Graph drawing by force-directed placement. *Software: Practice and experience, 21*(11), pp. 1129–1164. doi:10.1002/spe.4380211102

Garfield, E. (1970). Citation indexing for studying science. *Nature, 227*, pp. 669–671. doi:10.1038/ 227669a0

Geisler, E. (2000). *The metrics of science and technology*. Westport, CT: Quorum Books.

Godfrey, A., Thelwall, M., Enayat, M., & Power, G. (2008). *Generating new media and new participation in Iran: The case of ZigZag*. Stockholm, Sweden: International Association of Media and Communication Research.

Golder, S. A., & Huberman, B. A. (2006). The structure of collaborative tagging systems. *Journal of Information Science, 32*(2), pp. 198–208.

Gomes, B., & Smith, B. T. (2003). *Detecting query-specific duplicate documents*. U.S. Patent 6,615,209, retrieved from http://www.patents.com/Detecting-query-specific-duplicate-documents/ US6615209/en-US/.

Gyongyi, Z., Garcia-Molina, H., & Pedersen, J. (2004). Combating web spam with Trust-Rank. *Proceedings of the thirtieth international conference on Very large data bases, 30*, pp. 576–587.

Heimeriks, G., Hörlesberger, M., & van den Besselaar, P. (2003). Mapping communication and collaboration in heterogeneous research networks. *Scientometrics, 58*(2), pp. 391–413.

Heinonen, J., & Hägert, M. (2004). *Web metrics*, retrieved February 19, from http://web.abo.fi/ ~kaisa/HH.pdf.

Hinduja, S., & Patchin, J. W. (2008). Personal information of adolescents on the Internet: A quantitative content analysis of MySpace. *Journal of Adolescence, 31*(1), pp. 125–146. doi:10.1016/j.adolescence.2007.05.004

Holmberg, K., & Thelwall, M. (2009, to appear). Local government web sites in Finland: A geographic and webometric analysis. *Scientometrics, 79*(1), pp. 157–169. doi:10.1007/s11192-009-0410-6

Huntington, P., Nicholas, D., & Jamali, H. R. (2007). Site navigation and its impact on content viewed by the virtual scholar: A deep log analysis. *Journal of Information Science, 33*(5), pp. 598–610. doi:10.1177/0165551506077661

Ingwersen, P. (1998). The calculation of web impact factors. *Journal of Documentation, 54*(2), pp. 236–243. doi:10.1108/EUM0000000007167

Jascó, P. (2005). Google Scholar: The pros and the cons. *Online Information Review, 29*(2), pp. 208–214. doi:10.1108/14684520510598066

Kamada, T., & Kawai, S. (1989). An algorithm for drawing general undirected graphs. *Information Processing Letters, 31*(1), pp. 7–15. doi:10.1016/0020-0190(89)90102-6

Kleinberg, J. M. (1999). Authoritative sources in a hyperlinked environment. *Journal of the ACM, 46*(5), pp. 604–632. doi:10.1145/324133.324140

Kousha, K., & Thelwall, M. (2007). Google Scholar citations and Google Web/URL citations: A multi-discipline exploratory analysis. *Journal of the American Society for Information Science and Technology, 58*(7), pp. 1055–1065. doi:10.1002/asi.20584

Kousha, K., & Thelwall, M. (2008). Assessing the impact of disciplinary research on teaching: An automatic analysis of online syllabuses. *Journal of the American Society for Information Science and Technology, 59*(13), pp. 2060–2069. doi:10.1002/asi.20920

Latour, B., & Woolgar, S. (1979). *Laboratory life: The social construction of scientific facts*. Los Angeles: Sage.

Lawrence, S., & Giles, C. L. (1999). Accessibility of information on the web. *Nature, 400*(6740), pp. 107–109.

Lenhart, A., Arafeh, S., Smith, A., & Macgill, A. R. (2008). Writing, Technology and Teens (4/24/2008). *Pew Internet & American Life Project*, retrieved May 1, 2008, from http://www.pewinternet.org/PPF/r/2247/report_display.asp.

Li, X., Thelwall, M., Wilkinson, D., & Musgrove, P. B. (2005). National and international university departmental web site interlinking, part 2: Link patterns. *Scientometrics, 64*(2), pp. 187–208. doi:10.1007/s11192-005-0247-6

Liu, H. (2007). Social network profiles as taste performances. *Journal of Computer-Mediated Communication, 13*(1), retrieved June 5, 2008, from http://jcmc.indiana.edu/vol2013/issue2001/liu.html.

Mayr, P., & Tosques, F. (2005). Google Web APIs: An instrument for webometric analyses? Retrieved January 20, 2006, from http://www.ib.hu-berlin.de/%2007Emayr/arbeiten/ISSI2005_Mayr_Toques.pdf.

Mayr, P., & Walter, A. K. (2007). An exploratory study of Google Scholar. *Online Information Review, 31*(6), pp. 814–830. doi:10.1108/14684520710841784

McCowan, F., & Nelson, M. L. (2007). Search engines and their public interfaces: Which APIs are the most synchronized? *WWW 2007*, retrieved January 8, 2008, from http://www2007.org/htmlposters/poster2868/.

McEnery, T., & Wilson, A. (2001). *Corpus linguistics.* Edinburgh: Edinburgh University Press.

Merton, R. K. (1973). *The sociology of science. Theoretical and empirical investigations.* Chicago: University of Chicago Press.

Mettrop, W., & Nieuwenhuysen, P. (2001). Internet search engines—fluctuations in document accessibility. *Journal of Documentation, 57*(5), pp. 623–651.

Moed, H. F. (2005a). *Citation analysis in research evaluation.* New York: Springer.

Moed, H. F. (2005b). Statistical relationships between downloads and citations at the level of individual documents within a single journal (p). *Journal of the American Society for Information Science & Technology, 56*(10), pp. 1088–1097.

Neuendorf, K. (2002). *The content analysis guidebook.* London: Sage.

Newman, M. E. J. (2003). The structure and function of complex networks. *SIAM Review, 45*, pp. 167–256. doi:10.1137/S003614450342480

Nicolaisen, J. (2007). Citation analysis. *Annual Review of Information Science and Technology, 41*, pp. 609–641. doi:10.1002/aris.2007.1440410120

Ortega, J. L., Aguillo, I., Cothey, V., & Scharnhorst, A. (2008). Maps of the academic web in the European Higher Education Area: An exploration of visual web indicators. *Scientometrics, 74*(2), pp. 295–308. doi:10.1007/s11192-008-0218-9

Ortega, J. L., & Aguillo, I. F. (2008). Visualization of the Nordic academic web: Link analysis using social network tools. *Information Processing & Management, 44*(4), pp. 1624–1633. doi:10.1016/j.ipm.2007.09.010

Ortega, J. L., & Aguillo, I. F. (in press). Mapping world-class universities on the web. *Information Processing & Management, 45*(2), pp. 272–279.

Park, H. W., & Thelwall, M. (2006). Web science communication in the age of globalization: Links among universities' websites in Asia and Europe. *New Media and Society, 8*(4), pp. 631–652. doi:10.1177/1461444806065660

Pennock, D., Flake, G. W., Lawrence, S., Glover, E. J., & Giles, C. L. (2002). Winners don't take all: Characterizing the competition for links on the web. *Proceedings of the National Academy of Sciences, 99*(8), pp. 5207–5211. doi:10.1073/pnas.032085699

Rehm, G. (2002). *Towards automatic web genre identification*. Paper presented at the 35th Hawaii International Conference on System Sciences.

Rodríguez i Gairín, J. M. (1997). Valorando el impacto de la información en Internet: AltaVista, el "Citation Index" de la Red. *Revista Española de Documentación Científica, 20*(2), pp. 175–181.

Rogers, R. (2004). *Information politics on the web*. Massachusetts: MIT Press.

Rousseau, R. (1997). Sitations: an exploratory study. *Cybermetrics, 1*(1), retrieved July 25, 2006, from http://www.cindoc.csic.es/cybermetrics/articles/v2001i2001p2001.html.

Rousseau, R. (1999). Daily time series of common single word searches in AltaVista and Northern-Light. *Cybermetrics, 2/3*, retrieved July 25, 2006, from http://www.cindoc.csic.es/cybermetrics/articles/v2002i2001p2002.html.

Sherman, C., & Price, G. (2001). *The invisible web: Uncovering information sources search engines can't see*. Medford, NJ: Information Today.

Shifman, L., & Thelwall, M. (submitted for publication). Globalization under the radar: The worldwide diffusion of one Internet joke.

Smith, A. G. (1999). A tale of two web spaces; comparing sites using web impact factors. *Journal of Documentation, 55*(5), pp. 577–592.

Spink, A., & Jansen, B. J. (2004). *Web search: Public searching of the web*. Dordrecht: Kluwer Academic Publishers.

Srivastava, J., Cooley, R., Deshpande, M., & Tan, P.-N. (2000). Web Usage Mining: Discovery and applications of usage patterns from web data. *SIGKDD Explorations, 1*(2), pp. 12–23.

Stuart, D., & Thelwall, M. (2006). Investigating triple helix relationships using URL citations: A case study of the UK West Midlands automobile industry. *Research Evaluation, 15*(2), pp. 97–106. doi:10.3152/147154406781775968

Stuart, D., Thelwall, M., & Harries, G. (2007). UK academic web links and collaboration—an exploratory study. *Journal of Information Science, 33*(2), pp. 231–246. doi:10.1177/0165551506075326

Thelwall, M. (2001a). Exploring the link structure of the Web with network diagrams. *Journal of Information Science, 27*(6), pp. 393–402. doi:10.1177/016555150102700605

Thelwall, M. (2001b). Extracting macroscopic information from web links. *Journal of American Society for Information Science and Technology, 52*(13), pp. 1157–1168. doi:10.1002/asi.1182

Thelwall, M. (2001c). The responsiveness of search engine Indexes. *Cybermetrics, 5*(1), http://www.cindoc.csic.es/cybermetrics/articles/v5i1p1.html.

Thelwall, M. (2002a). Evidence for the existence of geographic trends in university web site interlinking. *Journal of Documentation, 58*(5), pp. 563–574. doi:10.1108/00220410210441586

Thelwall, M. (2002b). An initial exploration of the link relationship between UK university web sites. *ASLIB Proceedings, 54*(2), pp. 118–126. doi:10.1108/00012530210435248

Thelwall, M. (2003). What is this link doing here? Beginning a fine-grained process of identifying reasons for academic hyperlink creation. *Information Research, 8*(3), http://informationr.net/ir/8-3/paper151.html.

Thelwall, M. (2007). Blog searching: The first general-purpose source of retrospective public opinion in the social sciences? *Online Information Review, 31*(3), pp. 277–289. doi:10.1108/14684520710764069

Thelwall, M. (2008a). Extracting accurate and complete results from search engines: Case study Windows Live. *Journal of the American Society for Information Science and Technology, 59*(1), pp. 38–50. doi:10.1002/asi.20704

Thelwall, M. (2008b). Fk yea I swear: Cursing and gender in a corpus of MySpace pages. *Corpora, 3*(1), pp. 83–107.

Thelwall, M. (2008c). Quantitative comparisons of search engine results. *Journal of the American Society for Information Science and Technology, 59*(11), pp. 1702–1710. doi:10.1002/asi.20834

Thelwall, M. (2009). Homophily in MySpace. *Journal of the American Society for Information Science and Technology, 60*(2), pp. 219–231. doi:10.1002/asi.20978

Thelwall, M., & Harries, G. (2004). Do better scholars' web publications have significantly higher online impact? *Journal of American Society for Information Science and Technology, 55*(2), pp. 149–159.

Thelwall, M., & Hasler, L. (2007). Blog search engines. *Online Information Review, 31*(4), pp. 467–479. doi:10.1108/14684520710780421

Thelwall, M., & Prabowo, R. (2007). Identifying and characterising public science-related concerns from RSS feeds. *Journal of the American Society for Information Science & Technology, 58*(3), pp. 379–390.

Thelwall, M., & Price, L. (2006). Language evolution and the spread of ideas: A procedure for identifying emergent hybrid word family members. *Journal of the American Society for Information Science and Technology, 57*(10), pp. 1326–1337. doi:10.1002/asi.20437

Thelwall, M., Tang, R., & Price, E. (2003). Linguistic patterns of academic web use in Western Europe. *Scientometrics, 56*(3), pp. 417–432.

Thelwall, M., Vann, K., & Fairclough, R. (2006). Web issue analysis: An integrated water resource management case study. *Journal of the American Society for Information Science & Technology, 57*(10), pp. 1303–1314. doi:10.1002/asi.20434

Thelwall, M., & Wilkinson, D. (2003). Graph structure in three national academic Webs: Power laws with anomalies. *Journal of American Society for Information Science and Technology, 54*(8), pp. 706–712. doi:10.1002/asi.10267

Thelwall, M., & Zuccala, A. (2008). A university-centred European Union link analysis. *Scientometrics, 75*(3), pp. 407–420. doi:10.1007/s11192-007-1831-8

Trancer, B. (2008). *Click: What millions of people are doing online and why it matters.* London: Hyperion.

Vaughan, L. (2006). Visualizing linguistic and cultural differences using Web co-link data. *Journal of the American Society for Information Science and Technology, 57*(9), pp. 1178–1193. doi:10.1002/asi.20398

Vaughan, L., & Shaw, D. (2003). Bibliographic and Web citations: What is the difference? *Journal of the American Society for Information Science and Technology, 54*(14), pp. 1313–1322. doi:10.1002/asi.10338

Vaughan, L., & Shaw, D. (2005). Web citation data for impact assessment: A comparison of four science disciplines. *Journal of the American Society for Information Science & Technology, 56*(10), pp. 1075–1087. doi:10.1002/asi.20199

Vaughan, L., & Shaw, D. (2008). A new look at evidence of scholarly citation in citation indexes and from web sources. *Scientometrics, 74*(2), pp. 317–330. doi:10.1007/s11192-008-0220-2

Vaughan, L., & Thelwall, M. (2004). Search engine coverage bias: Evidence and possible causes. *Information Processing & Management, 40*(4), pp. 693–707. doi:10.1016/S0306-4573(03)00063-3

Vaughan, L., & Thelwall, M. (2005). A modeling approach to uncover hyperlink patterns: The case of Canadian universities. *Information Processing & Management, 41*(2), pp. 347–359. doi:10.1016/j.ipm.2003.10.001

Vaughan, L., & Wu, G. (2004). Links to commercial websites as a source of business information. *Scientometrics, 60*(3), pp. 487–496. doi:10.1023/B:SCIE.0000034389.14825.bc

Vaughan, L., & You, J. (2005). Mapping business competitive positions using Web co-link analysis. In P. Ingwersen & B. Larsen (Eds.), *Proceedings of 2005: The 10th International Conference of the International Society for Scientometrics and Informetrics* (pp. 534–543). Stockholm, Sweden: ISSI.

Wasserman, S., & Faust, K. (1994). *Social network analysis: Methods and applications.* Cambridge, NY: Cambridge University Press.

Zuccala, A. (2006). Author cocitation analysis is to intellectual structure as web colink analysis is to . . . ? *Journal of the American Society for Information Science & Technology, 57*(11), pp. 1487–1502. doi:10.1002/asi.20468

Author Biography

Michael Thelwall is professor of information science and leader of the Statistical Cybermetrics Research Group at the University of Wolverhampton, UK. He is also visiting fellow of the Amsterdam Virtual Knowledge Studio, a docent at Åbo Akademi University Department of Information Studies, and a research associate at the Oxford Internet Institute. He has developed tools for downloading and analyzing web sites, blogs, and social networking sites, including the research web crawler SocSciBot and software for statistical and topological analyses of site structures (through links) and site content (through text). He has published 145 refereed journal articles, seven book chapters, and the book *Link Analysis: An Information Science Approach*; is an associate editor of the *Journal of the American Society for Information Science and Technology*; and sits on eight other editorial boards. http://www.scit.wlv.ac.uk/~cm1993/mycv.html.